ALL ABOUT Spelling

The program that takes the struggle out of spelling

Level 1

by Marie Rippel

Copyright © 2014, 2006 by All About® Learning Press, Inc.
Printed in the United States of America

All About® Learning Press, Inc.
615 Commerce Loop
Eagle River, WI 54521

ISBN 978-1-935197-04-1
v. 1.8.0

Editor: Renée LaTulippe
Layout and Cover Design: Dave LaTulippe

The *All About Spelling* Level 1 Teacher's Manual is part of the *All About®* *Spelling* program.

For more books in this series, go to www.AllAboutSpelling.com.

To my mom, who gave me the love of words and knowledge. My mom provided a childhood for me filled with reading, studying, writing, and dreaming. I will never forget the wonder of a parcel of books delivered to our door one winter day, and my brother and sister and me draping ourselves over my mom while she read to us on the couch. As my mom's voice carried us along, the afternoon was transformed from dull and overcast to enchanting and unforgettable. It was soon after that I felt a determination to learn to put words on paper, and asked for a pencil…

Contents

A Quick Overview

This book is divided into three main sections:

1. **Preparing for Level 1.** In this section you will find **clear action steps** that will guide you as you prepare to teach *All About Spelling*. You will find information on what materials you need to gather, which letters and letter combinations will be taught, and how to set up your student's Spelling Review Box. The section also includes tips and suggestions for working with the letter tiles.

2. **Complete Step-by-Step Lesson Plans.** The second section contains easy-to-follow lesson plans for the twenty-four "Steps" that comprise Level 1. Each Step covers a main concept for your student to master, as well as review and reinforcement activities.

3. **Appendices.** The appendices contain extra information for your reference, such as the Scope and Sequence and a listing of all the words taught in Level 1.

For most students, I recommend working on spelling for twenty minutes a day, five days a week. Shorter, more frequent lessons are much more effective than longer, infrequent lessons.

If you have questions at any point, you can always reach me at support@allaboutlearningpress.com. I'm here to help!

Make spelling a joy!

Marie Rippel

1

Preparing for Level 1

Gather the Materials

Following is the list of materials you will need for teaching Level 1:

- ☐ Student Packet for Level 1
- ☐ Set of *All About Spelling* Letter Tiles
- ☐ *Phonogram Sounds* app
- ☐ Spelling Review Box or index card box
- ☐ Divider Cards
- ☐ Lined notebook paper

The following items are optional:

- ☐ Stickers or colored pencils for the Progress Chart
- ☐ Letter tile magnets
- ☐ 2' x 3' Magnetic white board

Get Ready for Multisensory Learning

During the learning process, we ideally use three main pathways to learning: **visual**, **auditory**, and **kinesthetic**.

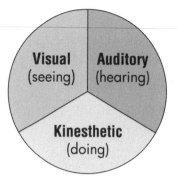

We are wired to learn using the three pathways, and the strength of each modality is different for each person. Some people may be very strong visual learners, while others learn best auditorily or kinesthetically. The *All About Spelling* program includes a variety of activities that use all three learning paths, because students achieve more when they are taught through their strongest pathway to the brain.

And here's the really good news. When students are taught using all three pathways to the brain—the visual, the auditory, and the kinesthetic—they learn even **more** than when they are taught only through their strongest pathway.[1]

You'll see that the spelling lessons in the pages ahead include various activities that engage all three pathways:

Visual
- watching as new spelling concepts are demonstrated with the color-coded letter tiles
- seeing the spelling words written down
- looking at and reading the flashcards during review sessions

Auditory
- reviewing the flashcards orally
- segmenting words aloud
- saying the sounds of the phonograms as they are written down

Kinesthetic
- writing down dictated phonograms, phrases, and sentences
- building new spelling words with the letter tiles
- practicing spelling with the pointer finger on various surfaces

Actively involving students in the spelling lessons through multisensory instruction like this speeds up the learning process.

---

[1]R. D. Farkus, "Effects of Traditional Versus Learning-Styles Instructional Methods on Middle School Students," *The Journal of Educational Research* 97, no. 1 (2003).

Get Ready for Multisensory Learning

Discover the Phonograms

A phonogram is a letter or letter combination that represents a sound. For example, the letter combination <u>ck</u> represents the sound /k/. The word *phonogram* comes from two Greek roots: *phono*, meaning *sound*, and *gram*, meaning *written*. Quite literally, then, a phonogram is a written sound.

Dr. Samuel Orton, a neurologist who studied language and reading disabilities, worked closely with teacher and psychologist Anna Gillingham to identify the sounds of the English language and the letter combinations used to represent those sounds. The *All About Spelling* program builds upon their extensive work in identifying the phonograms and how they are best taught.

The following chart lays out the basic phonograms.

a	b	c	d	e	f	g	h
i	j	k	l	m	n	o	p
qu	r	s	t	u	v	w	x
y	z	ai	ar	au	aw	ay	ch
ci	ck	dge	ea	ear	ed	ee	ei
eigh	er	ew	ey	gn	ie	igh	ir
kn	ng	nk	oa	oe	oi	oo	or
ou	ough	our	ow	oy	ph	sh	si
tch	th	ti	ui	ur	wh	wr	

In Level 1, through hands-on work with the letter tiles and continual review with the flashcards, your student will learn:

- the 32 unshaded phonograms in the chart above
- how to hear the individual sounds in words
- how to represent sounds using phonograms
- solid spelling rules governing the use of the phonograms

Learning these skills means that your student will not have to guess or memorize a string of letters in order to spell. The direct instruction in this program will give him real tools for mastering spelling.

Set Up the Spelling Review Box

The continual, individualized review featured in *All About Spelling* ensures that your students don't forget what you teach them and that they get the practice they need in exactly the areas they need it. Flashcards help accomplish much of this review, and the Spelling Review Box keeps them all organized.

Four types of flashcards will be used:

 These yellow cards offer **visual and verbal review**: you hold up the card and your student says the sound(s) the phonogram makes. Thirty-two Phonogram Cards are included with Level 1.

 Each red flashcard offers **aural and tactile review**: you dictate the sound and your student listens and writes the letter(s) that make the sound. Thirty-two Sound Cards are included with Level 1.

 Each blue flashcard contains a rule or generalization about spelling. These flashcards are used during lessons to **reinforce new concepts**: you read and review them with your student. Sixteen Key Cards are included with Level 1.

Each green flashcard contains a word that students learn to spell in Level 1. These cards offer **aural, verbal, and tactile review**: you dictate the word and your student listens to, segments, and writes the word.

Follow these steps to set up the Spelling Review Box:

1. Place the laminated divider cards (located in your Interactive Kit) in the Spelling Review Box in numerical order. We will refer to this important teaching tool as the **Spelling Review Box** throughout the series.

2. Separate the Phonogram Cards, Sound Cards, Key Cards, and Word Cards. Put all flashcards behind the appropriate Future Lessons dividers.

Did you know that a hundred years after the last wagon went over the Oregon Trail, you can still see the wagon ruts? Now that was a well-worn path! **This is what we want for our students: permanently ingrained learning.**

The *All About Spelling* program won't give your student time to forget anything. Continual review is so important that **each day's lesson begins with a review of previous material**. And you won't have to remember to do it, either, because the daily review is worked right into the lesson for you. We will keep treading that path until it is as permanent as the Oregon Trail—and you and your student will still see the effects years from now!

Familiarize Yourself with the Basic Phonograms

In Step 1, your student will learn the sounds of the first 26 phonograms, which correspond to the 26 letters of the alphabet. The following information is a guide to teaching this important first step.

Before introducing the flashcards in Step 1, make sure you know the sounds of the first 26 phonograms and can pronounce them clearly.

- Practice saying the pure sound without adding a noticeable /uh/ sound at the end. A common problem is to say /tuh/ instead of /t/, or /nuh/ instead of /n/.
- Listening to the *Phonogram Sounds* app is the quickest way to learn the sounds.

Download the *Phonogram Sounds* app. This free program for your computer, tablet, or phone features clear pronunciation of the sounds of all 72 basic phonograms (letters and letter combinations). Download the app at www.allaboutlearningpress.com/phonogram-sounds-app or scan the QR code. *(Note: If you'd prefer not to download the app, a CD-ROM version is available for purchase.)*

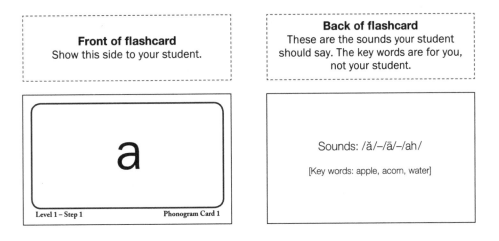

Front of flashcard
Show this side to your student.

a

Level 1 – Step 1   Phonogram Card 1

Back of flashcard
These are the sounds your student should say. The key words are for you, not your student.

Sounds: /ă/–/ā/–/ah/

[Key words: apple, acorn, water]

Some letters make more than one sound.

- Each sound will be written on the back of the flashcard. In the example above, you see that the letter <u>a</u> has three sounds.
- We always say the sounds in a particular order, starting with the most common sound.
- Say one sound after the other, with only a slight pause in between.

When a new phonogram is introduced, your student will learn all of the sounds of that phonogram at the same time.

- This method helps with recall because all of the sounds of that phonogram will be stored together in the student's brain.

All About Spelling is designed to work with how the student's mind naturally learns, and this is an important concept. Think of a filing cabinet: instead of tossing information in randomly, we are helping your student collect all of the information about the letters in one location and neatly file it away in the cabinet. When we enable the student to learn information in an orderly manner, the end result is greater learning.

A key word is printed on the back of each Phonogram Card.

- The key word is for your use only and will help trigger your memory when you are working with your student.
- You do not need to teach the word to your student.

We want students to make an instant connection between seeing the phonogram and saying the sound. Requiring key words such as "/n/ as in *nest*" or illustrating the phonograms with pictures will slow down the formation of that connection.

Some phonograms should not be taught together.

- Some phonograms sound alike to the untrained ear and to teach them together could result in confusion.
- The following sets of phonograms should be split up and taught in separate learning sessions:

b, d | a, e, i, o, u | p, b | m, n

- Wait until your student has mastered the first phonogram in each set before introducing the next.

Organize the Letter Tiles

Specially color-coded letter tiles are used to teach new spelling concepts in each lesson. This fantastic learning tool enables your student to learn to spell more quickly and accurately.

The *All About Spelling* letter tiles have many benefits:

- As the student works with the tiles, he internalizes the spelling concepts. When it comes time to spell with paper and pencil, he can be successful because he has already had practice.
- For remedial students, spelling with paper and pencil can become frustrating. Using the tiles provides a fresh start for them.
- The real power of the letter tiles is that they take an abstract thought and make it concrete. They turn an idea or concept into something your student can see and manipulate.

Organize the letter tiles as follows in preparation for teaching Level 1:

1. Separate the letter tiles and labels.
2. Label three plastic baggies **Use Now**, **Use Later**, and **Save for Level 2**. Sort the letter tiles and labels into the appropriate bags, as shown below.

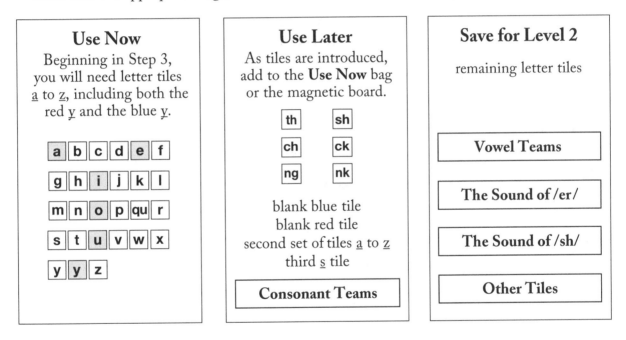

Use Now	**Use Later**	**Save for Level 2**
Beginning in Step 3, you will need letter tiles a to z, including both the red y and the blue y.	As tiles are introduced, add to the **Use Now** bag or the magnetic board. th sh ch ck ng nk blank blue tile blank red tile second set of tiles a to z third s tile **Consonant Teams**	remaining letter tiles **Vowel Teams** **The Sound of /er/** **The Sound of /sh/** **Other Tiles**

Consider using a magnetic white board during the spelling lessons.

Most teachers magnetize the letter tiles and store them on a magnetic white board. This is a great way to keep the tiles organized between lessons and to save time, too. If you opt to go this route, the following tips for preparing and using the letter tiles on a magnetic white board will help get you started.

- If you purchased the precut magnetic strips, simply peel off the paper backing and center one magnet on the back of each letter tile and two magnets on the back of each heading label. (The heading labels are the longer tiles with names such as "Consonant Teams," "Vowel Teams," and "The Sound of /er/.")

- The magnetic white board should be a minimum of 2' high by 3' wide. That will give you enough room for the full set of letters, plus plenty of open space to work in. You can go larger, of course, but it's not necessary.

- Before purchasing a board, check the product description to be sure it's actually magnetic. Boards may go by several names—magnet board, magnetic board, dry-erase board, white board, marker board—but magnets will not necessarily stick to all of them. Consider purchasing a board with a dry-erase feature—a nice addition to your daily lessons that offers yet another tactile way for your students to practice their spelling words.

- You can work with the letter tiles right on the magnetic white board, or remove just the letter tiles you need for the lesson and arrange them on the table.

Whether you work on the table or on a magnetic white board, the letter tiles should be set up in the same arrangement for each lesson. This will enable you and your student to quickly locate the letter tiles you need. When the letter tiles make their first appearance in Step 3, the setup consists of a single row of the letters <u>a</u> to <u>z</u>. More phonograms are introduced in this book and later in the series, and you will soon see the need for simple categories. To give you the big picture, here is the **letter tile layout after all the basic phonograms have been introduced:**

The graphic above shows what your letter tile layout will look like at the end of Level Five, after ALL the phonograms have been introduced. The first arrangement of letter tiles for Level 1, however, will be just one row of the 26 letter tiles, <u>a</u> to <u>z</u>.

Don't Forget! You should display only those letter tiles that have already been introduced in the lessons. Store the rest in the plastic baggies until you need them.

Six Steps to Teaching the AAS Method

The clear and logical layout of the lesson plans helps you see at a glance what you will be teaching each day. Everything is laid out for you in sequence.

Step 1. Read through each lesson before you teach it. Review any new phonograms or flashcards, and read the tips that you'll find sprinkled throughout the lesson.

Step 2. Gather the materials listed in the "You will need" section at the top of the lesson.

Step 3. With your student, review previously-taught concepts and materials. The flashcards will help you accomplish this essential first step.

| Review | Phonogram Cards | Sound Cards | Key Cards | Word Cards |

Step 4. Teach new concepts by simply following the script. Your teaching is shown in regular font, while the desired student response is shown in italics.

New Teaching	**Teach New Phonograms TH, SH, and CH**
	"We have three new tiles today."
	Point to the <u>sh</u> tile. `sh`
	"See how there are two letters on one tile? The two letters work together to make one sound. This one says /sh/. Repeat after me: /sh/." *Student repeats.*

Step 5. Reinforce new concepts through the dictation exercises provided.

Reinforcement	**Dictate Phrases**
	Dictate several phrases each day.
	step up
	felt hot
	fast sled
	wet frog

Step 6. File the flashcards. At the end of the lesson, file the flashcards behind the appropriate Review or Mastered dividers in your student's Spelling Review Box.

DON'T WORRY! You'll never be left to fend for yourself with *All About Spelling*. In addition to the tons of tips we've put right in the lesson plans, we've also provided little **"Don't Forget!"** reminders to keep your teaching on track. Your attention can be on your student instead of on figuring out how or what to teach.

Bring a Great Attitude!

Teaching your student can be a wonderful way to show him that he has great value in your eyes. You can view this as an opportunity to build him up and help him develop skill and character. Can you see yourself as a calm, uncritical coach with the worthy goal of helping this child fulfill his natural potential? Imagine the type of teacher *you* would want: friendly, supportive, with a you-can-do-it attitude. Smile. Point out what your student has done *right* more often than you point out his mistakes. Treat lesson time as a special time between the two of you.

Praise your student when he does well. We can get so used to correcting children that sometimes we overlook opportunities to let them know when they are doing something right. Listen to yourself to see if you need to fit in more expressions of approval. Here are some ideas to get you started:

"Wow, you catch on fast!"

"Excellent—you did so well!"

"Very good! You are a quick learner!"

"I love to work with you."

"Hey, you got that the first time!"

"You are doing great!"

"That was a tough one, and you got it!"

"Good for you!"

"You're getting it!"

"Awesome job!"

"You remembered that from yesterday—great!"

"I can tell that you tried hard to figure that out."

"Way to go!"

"Just last week you couldn't have done that!"

> *"Kind words can be short and easy to speak,*
> *but their echoes are truly endless."*
> –Mother Teresa

2

Complete Step-by-Step
Lesson Plans

Following are twenty-four Steps. Each Step contains a major concept that needs to be mastered by the student in order to form a strong foundation for spelling. Schedule as many (or as few!) study sessions as your student needs in order to understand the concept in each Step.

Steps 1, 2, and 3 contain pre-spelling skills that can be worked on simultaneously. After that, each Step needs to be mastered before moving on to the next one.

Step 1 – The First 26 Phonograms

In this lesson, your student will learn the sounds of the first 26 phonograms.

You will need: Phonogram Cards 1-26, Progress Chart

Before beginning this lesson, read "Familiarize Yourself with the Basic Phonograms" on page 9 for important background information.

This step has two main components:
1. Figuring out which phonograms need to be taught.
2. Teaching the phonograms.

Evaluation

Determine which Phonograms Need to Be Taught

Take out Phonogram Cards 1 to 26.

"We are going to see which of these cards you know and which of them we should work on. We will sort them into two piles: *cards you know* and *cards you need to learn*."

Show your student the front side of Phonogram Card 2.

"Most letters have one sound. For example, the letter <u>b</u> says /b/." Return the card to the back of the deck.

Show your student the front side of Phonogram Card 1.

"But some letters can say *more* than one sound, depending on the word it is found in. For example, the letter <u>a</u> can say /ă/, or it can say /ā/, or it can say /ah/, depending on the word."

"When I show you a letter that can say more than one sound, tell me *all* of the sounds. For this card, you would say /ă/–/ā/–/ah/." Return the card to the back of the deck.

Go through all of the Phonogram Cards with your student and sort them into two piles: **Need to Learn** and **Mastered**.

When you get to Phonogram Card 17, you may need to give the following explanation to your student:

"You can see that there are two letters on this card. In English, q is always followed by a u. Together, they say the sound of /kw/. Repeat after me: /kw/."

What is considered a mastered card? These are the cards that your student knows thoroughly. He says the pure, clipped sound without adding /uh/ at the end—for example, he says /p/, not /puh/. He can respond quickly and easily when you hold up the card and does not hesitate to think of the answer. There is no doubt in your mind that he has, in fact, mastered the card.

If there are any cards in the Mastered pile at the end of the evaluation, file them behind the **Phonogram Cards Mastered** divider. Mastered cards will be reviewed periodically throughout the program.

New Teaching

Don't Forget! When saying the sounds of phonograms that have multiple sounds, remember to say one sound after the other with only a slight pause in between. For the letter c, for example, you would say "/k/ – /s/," pausing momentarily between the sounds. The *Phonogram Sounds* app demonstrates how to do this.

Teach the Phonograms

Now that you have identified which cards your student needs to learn, teach four cards at a time with the following procedure:

1. Show the Phonogram Card.
2. Say the sound or sounds.
3. Have your student repeat the sound or sounds.

If a phonogram has several sounds, you can give your student a "hint" by holding up the appropriate number of fingers.

After several repetitions, see if your student can say the sound(s) without your prompting. The goal is that as you flip through the flashcards, your student will be able to say the phonograms without pausing to think.

New Teaching

(continued)

File the four Phonogram Cards that you are working on behind the **Phonogram Cards Review** divider in your student's Spelling Review Box. They will be reviewed at the beginning of the next teaching session.

After your student has mastered the Phonogram Cards, you will move them behind the **Phonogram Cards Mastered** divider.

Keep Track of which Phonograms Have Been Learned

Take out the Phonogram Chart.

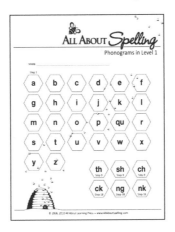

Have your student color in or place a sticker next to the phonograms that have been mastered.

Update this chart each time a Phonogram Card is moved to the Mastered pile.

How many phonograms should you teach in a day?
For some students, especially younger ones, learning four new Phonogram Cards at a time will be enough. Other students, especially those who are good readers, will be able to learn many more in a day. You will have to judge the attention span and previous experience of your student and adjust the number of cards to teach in a session. You don't want to frustrate your student by trying to teach too many in a day, yet you don't want to hold him back by not teaching *enough*, either.

Tip!

Reinforcement

Mark the Progress Chart

Post the Progress Chart in an accessible area. After each Step has been completed, have your student color in or place a sticker over that Step number on the chart.

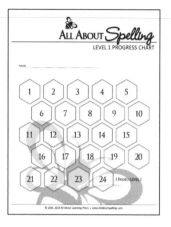

Step 2 – Segmenting Words

This lesson will teach how to segment words containing up to three sounds.

You will need: three tokens (colored disks)

When we speak, we blend sounds together very quickly to form words. To say the word *ham*, for instance, we blend the sounds /h/–/ă/–/m/.

Segmenting is the opposite of blending. When we segment a word, we say each individual sound separately.

In this lesson, your student will learn how to hear the sounds in short words so that later he can represent each sound with a written phonogram. A student who can segment words into their basic sounds can spell much more easily.

Review

Continual review is an essential part of learning to spell. At the beginning of each Step, you will find a Review section like this one. The graphics indicate the material that you should review with your student before you move on to the New Teaching section.

Don't Forget!

In this case, the graphic above indicates that you should review the Phonogram Cards from Step 1 that you filed behind the Review divider in your student's Spelling Review Box.

New Teaching

Repeat the First Sound in a Word

You will be asking your student to repeat the **first sound** in a word.

You are not asking for the name of the first letter; **you are asking for the first sound.**

For example, the first **sound** in the word *map* is /m/. Your student, therefore, should respond by saying /m/, not *the letter m*.

Turn toward your student so he can see your mouth as you speak.

"The first sound we hear in the word *floor* is /f/. What is the first sound you hear in the word *sun*?" /s/.

"What is the first sound you hear in the word *ball*?" /b/.

Repeat this exercise as many times as necessary until it becomes easy for your student. Use the words below:

fan	lamp	map	stamp	van
rug	book	help	paint	grass
wall	beach	yarn	desk	jump
hose	zoo	tent	run	paper
cabin	dig	girl	lemon	name

If your student needs extra help, try these strategies:

Tip!

• Hold or exaggerate the first sound of the word.

• Make sure your student watches your mouth.

• Have your student say the word s-l-o-w-l-y, and then go back and repeat the first sound he said.

Repeat the Last Sound in a Word

"Now you are going to say the *last* sound in a word. The last sound in the word *jam* is /m/. Repeat the last sound in the word *glass*." /s/.

Repeat this exercise as many times as necessary until it becomes easy for your student. Use the words below:

tree	run	egg	pop	feet
home	class	maze	book	rob
free	road	sleep	seat	wall
hot	if	moon	hill	may
off	horse	robe	rock	wave

Step 2: Segmenting Words

Segment Words with Two Sounds

 For the segmenting activities in this lesson, you can either use coins or the round tokens that were included in your Level 1 Student Packet.

Don't Forget! The student should not yet be using the letter tiles, which will be introduced in Step 3.

Make sure your student uses his **dominant hand** for activities involving tokens and letter tiles.

Lay two tokens on the table. Using the lists below, give your student a word that has two sounds. The student should repeat the word and then say the individual sounds. **As he says each sound**, he pulls a token toward himself, like this:

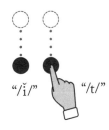

"/ĭ/"   "/t/"

In this activity, the student is not writing the word. He is orally segmenting the word, using tokens to represent each sound.

Begin the activity with the following list of words, all of which have initial sounds that are easy to "hold," as in *ssss-ee, rrrr-ow,* and *mmmm-ay.* These words will be simpler for your student to segment into their separate sounds. Repeat the exercise until it becomes easy for your student.

see	row	may	say	at
zoo	is	in	me	so
on	as	Sue	we	of
no	fee	oat	it	knee
Ann	eat	lie	am	

Make sure that your student says the sound as he pulls down the corresponding token. We will build upon this routine in later lessons. Tip!

Continue the activity with the following words, which have initial sounds that are not as easy to hold.

go	pay	key	to	pie
hoe	do	hi	by	he
hay	be	tea	tie	day

Once your student can easily segment words with two sounds, continue on to this next activity.

Tip!

Segment Words with Three Sounds

Lay three tokens on the table. Give your student a word that has three sounds. The student should repeat the word and then say the individual sounds. **As he says each sound**, he pulls a token toward himself, like this:

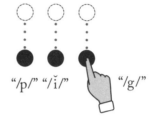

"/p/" "/ĭ/"   "/g/"

Repeat this exercise until it becomes easy for your student.

pig	mat	hot	red	map
bed	rat	wet	sit	led
big	mop	ten	lid	fed
ran	dad	tip	fan	get
bus	log	mud	jam	men
pet	Tom	win	set	sad
rag	yes	met	nod	hop
lip	did	leg	tan	nap
bug	bat	rib	zip	mom
him	run	man	bit	gum
sun	hug	hit	dog	hip

Step 3 – The Letter Tiles

This lesson will introduce the letter tiles, teach how to alphabetize them, and teach how to identify vowels and consonants.

You will need: three tokens, letter tiles <u>a</u> to <u>z</u> including both the blue <u>y</u> and the red <u>y</u>, Key Cards 1 and 2

Review

Phonogram Cards

Don't Forget!

At the beginning of each lesson, review the cards behind the **Review** dividers in your student's Spelling Review Box. This only takes a few minutes, but it makes a big difference in your student's long-term retention.

If your student has mastered a card, file it behind the appropriate **Mastered** divider.

Segment Words

Set out three tokens. Have your student segment the following words aloud, pulling down a token for each sound.

ten   **pan**   **hot**   **gum**   **sit**

New Teaching

Introduce the Letter Tiles

Show your student the letter tiles and place the <u>b</u> tile in front of him.

b

"These letter tiles contain the same letters as the flashcards. Can you tell me the sound that this tile makes?" */b/.*

Point out several more tiles and ask your student to identify them.

New Teaching
(continued)

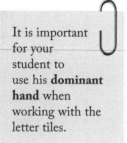

It is important for your student to use his **dominant hand** when working with the letter tiles.

Teach How to Alphabetize the Letter Tiles

Lay out letter tiles a to z in random order, keeping the extra red y letter tile off to the side for use later in the lesson. Teach your student how to alphabetize the letter tiles. He can sing the alphabet song if necessary.

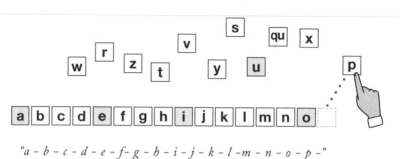

"a – b – c – d – e – f– g – h – i – j – k – l –m – n – o – p –"

> **You and your student will work together to put the letter tiles in order at the beginning of each lesson.** He may **Tip!** be slow at first—that's okay; he'll get faster with practice. The two of you will soon be able to set up the tiles in a minute.
>
> **As your student gains experience with alphabetizing, you can model for him how to start from different points in the alphabet song.** This is useful if the letter tiles are laid out up through m, for example. Instead of starting the song from the beginning, he can start from l.
>
> **Eventually your student will be able to set up the letter tiles as they come out of the bag.** Tell him that the m and n are in the middle of the alphabet, so when he gets those tiles, set them in the middle. As he gets each tile, he should decide if it is in the first half or second half of the alphabet.

Don't Forget! Key Cards contain rules and generalizations about spelling. We use them to reinforce and review new concepts to keep them fresh in your student's mind.

Teach Key Cards 1 and 2: Vowels and Consonants

"Some of the letter tiles are red. These are the vowels."

"The rest of the letter tiles are blue. These are the consonants."

Bring out the red y tile.   y   y

"The letter y can be a vowel or a consonant. When it says /y/, it is a consonant. When it says /ĭ/, /ī/ or /ē/, it is a vowel."

New Teaching
(continued)

Take out Key Card 1 and read it with your student.

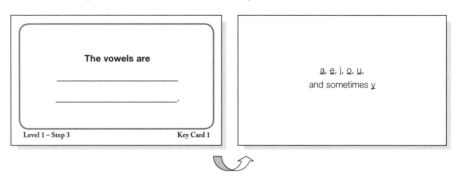

Take out Key Card 2 and read it with your student.

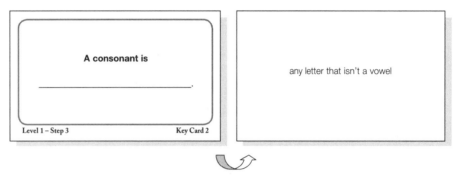

"B is a consonant. L is a consonant." Point to the letter tiles as you mention them.

"Can you tell me some other consonants?" *Student names some consonants.*

File Key Cards 1 and 2 behind the **Key Cards Review** divider. They will be reviewed daily.

After your student has mastered the Key Cards, you will move them behind the **Key Cards Mastered** divider.

Step 4 – The Sound Cards

This lesson will teach how to write the phonograms.

You will need: three tokens, Sound Cards 1-26

Review

You'll notice that for this lesson you will be reviewing both Phonogram Cards and Key Cards. In later lessons, you will add Sound Cards and Word Cards to your daily review.

Segment Words

Set out three tokens. Have your student segment the following words aloud, pulling down a token for each sound:

job **tan** **mug** **pin** **rat**

Alphabetize the Letter Tiles

Starting with this step, always alphabetize the letter tiles with your student at the beginning of each lesson.

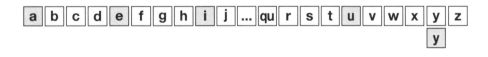

New Teaching

Introduce the Sound Cards

Take out Sound Cards 1 to 26. Shuffle the deck.

For this activity, students will only indicate the letter tile, rather than write the letter.

"I am going to dictate a sound, and you will point to the letter tile that makes that sound."

New Teaching
(continued)

Dictate the Sound Cards. The student should not see the front of the card.

Practice until your student can easily match up the correct letter tile with the sound.

This is usually an easy activity for students who know the Phonogram Cards. If it does not come easily for your student, however, here is a suggestion:

Choose four or five Sound Cards to work with at first. Put the corresponding letter tiles in front of your student. Now when you dictate the sound, your student will have a limited number of letter tiles from which to choose. As he catches on, add more Sound Cards and letter tiles.

Teach Sound Cards 1-26: Writing the Phonograms from Dictation

The student will need lined paper and pencil. Show him how to fold his paper in half lengthwise to form two columns. He should write one phonogram per line.

Adjust the number of Sound Cards you dictate in each session according to your student's ability. With younger students you may choose to practice only a few per day, while with older students you may be able to go through the deck several times.

"I am going to dictate a sound. Instead of pointing to the letter tile, you will write the letter that makes the sound."

Dictate the Sound Cards. The student should repeat the sound(s) as he writes the phonogram.

File the flashcards behind the **Sound Cards Review** divider in your student's Spelling Review Box. They will be reviewed daily.

After your student has mastered the Sound Cards, you will move them behind the **Sound Cards Mastered** divider.

New Teaching

(continued)

It is important for the student to say the sounds of the phonograms as he writes them down. Doing so involves the three pathways to the brain: visual (seeing the phonogram), auditory (hearing the phonogram spoken aloud), and kinesthetic (feeling the process of forming the letters and feeling the vocal cords as the sound is repeated).

To maximize the kinesthetic aspect and provide interesting review, have your student "write" on one of the tactile surfaces below. The student should use his pointer finger instead of a pencil and write in large letters.

- Sand in a shoe box lid
- A sheet of very fine sandpaper
- "Feely" fabrics such as burlap, velvet, or corduroy
- Rice poured into a baking pan
- Plush carpet square

These next items can be put into a sealed plastic baggie to create a no-mess surface, and your student can use his finger to write through the bag.

- Shaving cream
- Pudding (This one you can eat after the lesson!)
- Liquid soap
- Glue

Practice over as many sessions as necessary until your student can easily write down the dictated phonograms.

Step 5 – Short Vowels

This lesson will teach the short vowel sounds and how to choose the correct vowel.

You will need: three tokens, Key Cards 3 and 4, a blank red tile, Phonogram Cards 1, 5, 9, 15, and 21

In this lesson we will concentrate on the short vowel sounds. As you know, the vowels each have more than one sound. The letter e, for example, has two sounds. The first sound, /ĕ/, we call short e. Your student will learn that the first sound of each vowel is called its short sound.

We are concentrating on the short sounds because they are the most frequently used of the vowel sounds. It is important that your student be able to choose the correct vowel when he hears it in a word.

Review

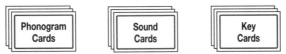

Segment Words

Set out three tokens. Have your student segment the following words aloud, pulling down a token for each sound:

ham   **zip**   **rob**   **tug**   **bed**

 Alphabetize letter tiles a to z with your student at the beginning of every lesson. Organized letter tiles make for smooth lessons!

Don't Forget! Always lay out **only** the tiles that have already been introduced. At this point, you need only letter tiles a to z.

New Teaching   Teach Key Card 3: Short Vowel Sounds

Pull down letter tiles a, e, i, o, and u.

New Teaching
(continued)

"I am going to dictate a vowel sound, and you will point to the vowel that makes that sound. Usually, I dictate all of the sounds the vowel makes, but today I am only going to say the first sound the vowel makes. See if you can figure it out."

"/ă/." [as in *apple*]   *Student points to the a tile.*

"/ŭ/." [as in *up*]   *Student points to the u tile.*

"/ĕ/." [as in *end*]   *Student points to the e tile.*

"/ĭ/." [as in *igloo*]   *Student points to the i tile.*

"/ŏ/." [as in *odd*]   *Student points to the o tile.*

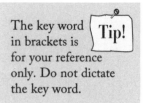

The key word in brackets is for your reference only. Do not dictate the key word.

Practice until your student can easily match up the correct tile with the sound.

Take out Phonogram Cards 1, 5, 9, 15, and 21. These are the cards for the vowels.

Hold up Phonogram Card 1.

"What sounds does this letter make?" */ă/–/ā/–/ah/.*

"Good. The first sound you said, /ă/, is called the **short sound of a.**"

Hold up Phonogram Card 5.

"What sounds does this letter make?" */ĕ/–/ē/.*

"Good. The first sound you said, /ĕ/, is called the **short sound of e.**"

Repeat this activity with Phonogram Cards 9, 15, and 21 so that the student can see that the first sound is the short sound.

Practice Key Card 3 with your student until the activity becomes easy. File the card behind the Review divider.

Repeat after me: A vowel's first sound is short.
(Student repeats.)
Point to the vowel that says...

/ă/   [as in *apple*]
/ĕ/   [as in *end*]
/ĭ/   [as in *igloo*]
/ŏ/   [as in *odd*]
/ŭ/   [as in *up*]

Level 1 – Step 5   Key Card 3

Each day, dictate the short vowel sounds in a different order. Have your student point to the correct letter tile.

Do not dictate the key word.

Step 5: Short Vowels

Choose the Correct Vowel

Build the word *mat* with the tiles, using a blank red tile in place of the vowel.

m		t

"I want to spell the word *mat*. What sound will go here?" Point to the blank tile. */ă/.*

"Good. I will take out the blank tile and put in the tile that says /ă/."

m	a	t

Build the word *pet* with the tiles, using a blank red tile in place of the vowel.

p		t

"Now it is your turn. Spell the word *pet*." *Student replaces the blank tile with the e tile.*

p	e	t

Repeat this activity as many times as necessary until it becomes easy for your student. Use the following words, replacing the vowel with a blank red tile.

l__d ➔ "Spell the word **lid**."

h__m ➔ "Spell the word **ham**."

m__d ➔ "Spell the word **mud**."

p__t ➔ "Spell the word **pot**."

qu__t ➔ "Spell the word **quit**."

z__p ➔ "Spell the word **zip**."

b__d ➔ "Spell the word **bad**."

f__n ➔ "Spell the word **fan**."

h__d ➔ "Spell the word **hid**."

m__p ➔ "Spell the word **mop**."

h__m ➔ "Spell the word **hum**."

l__g ➔ "Spell the word **leg**."

n__t ➔ "Spell the word **net**."

j__g ➔ "Spell the word **jog**."

t__g ➔ "Spell the word **tug**."

w__b ➔ "Spell the word **web**."

s__t ➔ "Spell the word **sit**."

Teach Key Card 4: Every Word Has a Vowel

"Did you notice that every word we made had a red tile—a vowel?" Build some words from the previous activity to demonstrate this rule.

Read Key Card 4 with your student and then file it behind the Review divider.

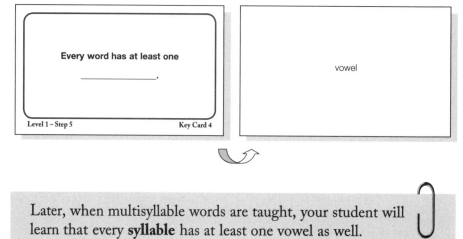

Later, when multisyllable words are taught, your student will learn that every **syllable** has at least one vowel as well.

Exchange Vowels to Make New Words

Build the word *hit* with the tiles. [h] [i] [t]

"This word is *hit*. I can change this word to *hot* like this."

"Now it is your turn. This word is *run*." [r] [u] [n]

"Change it to the word *ran* by switching one of the tiles."
Student exchanges the u for an a tile.

New Teaching
(continued)

Repeat this activity as many times as necessary until it becomes easy for your student. Using the following sets of words, build the first word and have your student change it to the word you specify.

pan → pin → pen

mat → met

map → mop

sat → sit → set

cat → cut

cap → cup

tap → tip → top

rug → rag

hum → ham → him → hem

red → rod → rid

hot → hit → hut → hat

got → get

lot → lit

log → leg

dig → dog

big → bag → beg → bug

tag → tug

bat → bit

Step 6 – Short A

In this lesson, your student will learn how to segment words using letter tiles and how to spell words with short a.

You will need: three tokens, Word Cards 1-10

Up until now, your student has been segmenting words using tokens to represent each sound. In this Step, we are going to review that activity once again and then move on to segmenting words using letter tiles. Once segmenting with tiles becomes easy for your student, he will be ready to move on to spelling.

Review

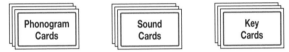

Segment Words

Set out three tokens. Have your student segment the following words aloud, pulling down a token for each sound:

| mud | bit | van | hem | mom |

New Teaching

Teach How to Segment with Tiles

Set the tokens aside and put the following letter tiles in a row in front of your student: <u>a</u>, <u>r</u>, <u>t</u>.

"Today you will spell a word using the letter tiles."

"I will say a word and you will repeat it slowly, one sound at a time, like you did with the tokens. Instead of pulling down a **token** for each sound, you will choose the correct **letter tile** and pull it down."

"The word is *rat*." Point to the letter tiles. *Student segments the word aloud, pulling down the correct letter tile for each sound.*

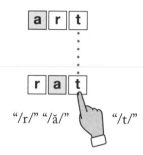

"Read the word you just spelled." *Rat.*

Put the following letter tiles in a row in front of your student: <u>a</u>, <u>b</u>, <u>c</u>, <u>d</u>, <u>e</u>, <u>f</u>, <u>g</u>.

a b c d e f g

The chart on the next page summarizes this procedure for spelling with letter tiles. We will continue to use this routine throughout Level 1.

"This time you will have more letters to choose from."

"The word is *bad*." Point to the letter tiles. *Student segments the word aloud, pulling down the correct letter tile for each sound.*

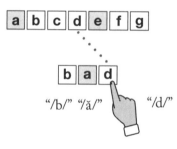

"Read the word you just spelled." *Bad.*

"Good. Now put the letters back in order." *Student does so.*

If your student needs more practice with this concept, use the following words. Gradually increase the number of letters available for him to choose from.

jam	lap	bag	fan	pat
tap	rag	bat	wag	ham
dad	tag	nap	fat	sad
mad	cat	van	bad	ram
mat	rat			

Step 6: Short A

New Teaching
(continued)

You just walked your student through the **Procedure for Spelling with Tiles**. We will use this routine throughout Level 1. Each of the four steps is important.

1 **Dictate the word, then point to the tiles.**

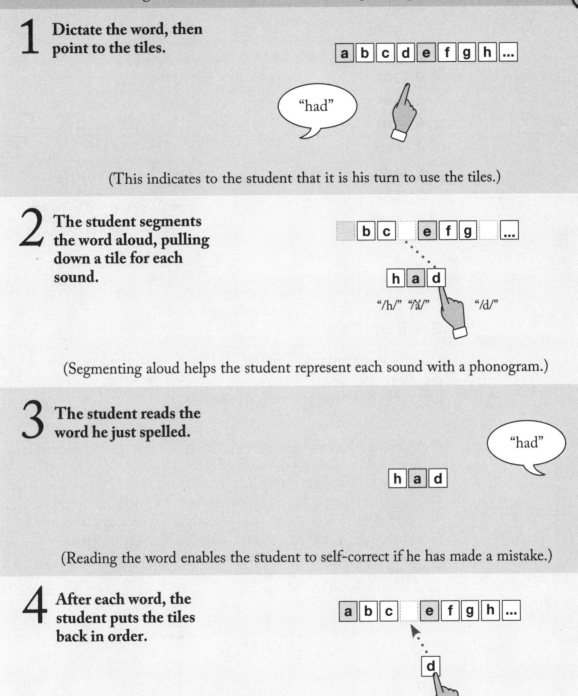

(This indicates to the student that it is his turn to use the tiles.)

2 **The student segments the word aloud, pulling down a tile for each sound.**

(Segmenting aloud helps the student represent each sound with a phonogram.)

3 **The student reads the word he just spelled.**

(Reading the word enables the student to self-correct if he has made a mistake.)

4 **After each word, the student puts the tiles back in order.**

(Returning the tiles to the correct order reinforces alphabetizing skills and keeps the workspace organized.)

Word Cards 1-10: Spell with Tiles

Dictate the words and have your student spell them with tiles. Use the **Procedure for Spelling with Tiles** on the previous page.

1. **at**
2. **man**
3. **sat**
4. **am**
5. **an**   Is that an octopus?
6. **ran**
7. **had**
8. **hat**
9. **gas**
10. **map**

Working with the Word Cards provides essential aural, verbal, and tactile practice for your student.

Don't Forget!

Be sure your student follows the Procedure for Spelling with Tiles as you dictate each word.

If your student has a hard time distinguishing between *am* and *an* when you dictate the words, have him watch your lips.

If a spelling word has a homophone—another word that sounds alike but is spelled differently—dictate the word in a sentence for clarity. **The student does not write the sentence.**

Spell on Paper

Once your student is able to spell the words using the letter tiles, dictate Word Cards 1-10 and have him spell the words on lined paper. He should write one word per line.

As a general rule, keep the most recently learned flashcards behind the Word Cards Review divider. Reviewing them at the beginning of the next lesson will help you better determine if your student has really mastered those cards. It often seems as if a student has mastered a card during the spelling lesson—but when you revisit that card in a day or two, it becomes obvious that he really hasn't.

More Words

The following words reinforce the concepts taught in Step 6. Have your student spell them for additional practice.

bad	**bag**	**bat**	**cat**
dad	**fan**	**fat**	**ham**
jam (grape jam)	**lap**	**lab**	**mad**
mat (welcome mat)	**nap**	**pad**	**pat**
rag	**ram**	**rat**	**sad**
tag	**tap**	**van**	**wag**

You will be seeing **More Words** in each Step that includes a spelling list. There are two different ways you can use the **More Words** section. Tailor it to meet your student's needs.

Tip!

Method #1: Have your student read the list. Point out that he can now spell these words, as well as the words he learned from the spelling list. Dictate several of the words to make sure that he can apply the concept taught in the lesson to new words.

This method works well with most older students and advanced younger students. They are introduced to the words they are able to spell and can quickly move on to the next step. They are not held back with unnecessary repetition.

Method #2: Teach the words in the same manner as you did the words on the main spelling list.

This method works well with younger students and with older students who struggle with spelling. They gain the extra practice they need with a concept instead of being pushed ahead before they are ready.

The **More Words** section dramatically expands the number of words that your student learns. Instead of knowing just the ten words that were given on the spelling list, he knows many more because he is learning the concepts behind spelling.

Step 7 – Short I

In this lesson, your student will learn words containing short i.

You will need: Word Cards 11–20, extra <u>d</u> letter tile

Remember to alphabetize the letter tiles at the beginning of each lesson. Today you will set out an extra <u>d</u> letter tile so your student can spell the word *did*.

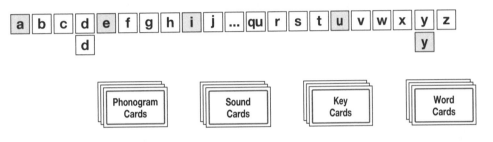

Review

Shuffle and review the cards behind the Review dividers daily. This gives your student practice with a variety of spelling concepts presented in random order.

New Teaching

If your student misspells the word, have him read the word exactly as he spelled it. Help him determine which letter is incorrect, and then have him spell the word correctly.

Practice the Procedure for Spelling with Tiles

"I will dictate a word, and you will spell it using the letter tiles."

"The word is *pig*." Point to the row of letter tiles to prompt your student to begin using the tiles.

Student segments the word *pig*, pulling down the letter tiles as he says the sounds. /p/–/i/–/g/.

"Read the word." *Pig.*

"Good!"

Word Cards 11-20: Spell with Tiles

Dictate the words and have your student spell them with tiles. Follow the **Procedure for Spelling with Tiles**, illustrated in Appendix C.

11. in   She's in big trouble!
12. big
13. hit
14. pig
15. him   I told him a secret.
16. sit
17. did
18. it
19. if
20. dig

Spell on Paper

Once your student is able to spell the words using the tiles, dictate Word Cards 11-20 and have him spell the words on paper.

File the Word Cards behind the Review divider.

More Words

The following words reinforce the concepts taught in Step 7. Have your student spell them for additional practice.

bit	**dim**	**fit**	**hid**
hip	**lid**	**lip**	**pin**
pit	**rib**	**rip**	**tip**
win	**zip**		

Step 7: Short I

Step 8 – Short O

This lesson will teach how to capitalize proper names and how to spell words containing short o.

You will need: Key Card 5, Word Cards 21-30, extra m letter tile

Review

Phonogram Cards   Sound Cards   Key Cards   Word Cards

New Teaching

Teach Key Card 5: Capitalization

Read Key Card 5 with your student and file behind the Review divider.

Names start with a

Level 1 – Step 8   Key Card 5

capital letter

Demonstrate this concept by writing names on paper for your student to see: *Bob, Dan, Ron.* Your student will put this into practice with the names in the Reinforcement section of this lesson.

Practice the Procedure for Spelling with Tiles

"I will dictate a word, and you will spell it using the letter tiles."

"The word is *top.*" Point to the row of letter tiles to prompt your student to begin using the tiles.

Student segments the word *top*, pulling down the letter tiles as he says the sounds. /t/–/o/–/p/.

t o p

"Read the word." *Top.*

"Good!"

Remember, if your student misspells the word, have him read the word exactly as he spelled it. Help him determine which letter is incorrect, and then have him spell the word correctly.

Word Cards 21-30: Spell with Tiles

Dictate the words and have your student spell them with tiles. Follow the **Procedure for Spelling with Tiles**, illustrated in Appendix C.

21. on
22. not   He does not like cake.
23. mom
24. hot
25. got
26. dog
27. top
28. log
29. job
30. hop

Pronounce for Spelling

There are regional variations in how we pronounce some words. In the above list, your student may pronounce *dog* as *dawg* and *log* as *lawg*. If so, tell your student to "pronounce the word for spelling."

There will be other times when we'll need to "pronounce for spelling"—that is, to pronounce the word clearly and as it is written. This concept becomes especially important in higher levels. Take the word *button*. Most of us say *butn*. The vowel sound in the unaccented syllable gets lost in the normal rhythm of speech. But in order to spell it, it is helpful to "pronounce for spelling" and enunciate each syllable clearly: *but-ton*.

Reinforcement

Spell on Paper

Once your student is able to spell the words using the tiles, dictate Word Cards 21-30 and have him spell the words on paper.

File the Word Cards behind the Review divider.

More Words

The following words reinforce the concepts taught in Step 8. Have your student spell them for additional practice.

Bob	**Dan**	**dot**	**fog**
God	**Jim** (Uncle Jim) **jog**		**lot**
mop	**Pam**	**pod**	**pop**
pot	**rob**	**Ron**	**rot**
Sam	**sob**	**sod**	**Tom**

If your student misspells a word during a lesson, there are several things you should do:

Tip!

1. **Ask the student to slowly read exactly what he has written down.**
   Often the student will see his own error and be able to fix it.

2. **Take a look at what caused the mistake.**
   Does he pronounce the word incorrectly?
   Do you need to re-teach something?
   Did he segment the word incorrectly?

   If you need to review a Key Card or Sound Card related to the misspelling, do it now.

3. **Have the student spell the word again, first with tiles and then on paper.**

Customizing your student's instruction in this way will help him grow in spelling ability more quickly.

Reinforcement

(continued)

 How is the daily review going? Are the decks behind the Mastered dividers getting bigger?

Mastered cards will be reviewed in Step 11 to keep them fresh in your student's mind.

Step 9 – Short U

This lesson will teach three new phonograms and how to spell words containing short u.

You will need: letter tiles <u>th</u>, <u>sh</u>, and <u>ch</u>, Consonant Teams label, Phonogram Cards 27-29, Sound Cards 27-29, Word Cards 31-40

Before teaching your student today, review the new Phonogram Cards that you will be presenting in the lesson.

The phonograms <u>th</u>, <u>sh</u>, and <u>ch</u> are **digraphs**. Digraphs are two letters that make one sound.

Review

 Are you remembering to shuffle the Word Cards before dictating them? Dictate review words with a variety of patterns.

New Teaching

Teach New Phonograms TH, SH, and CH

"We have three new tiles today."

Point to the <u>th</u> tile.

"See how there are two letters on one tile? The two letters work together to make one sound. This one can say /th/, or it can say /t̶h̶/. Repeat after me: /th/–/t̶h̶/." *Student repeats the sounds.*

Point to the <u>sh</u> tile.

"This one says /sh/. Repeat after me: /sh/." *Student repeats the sound.*

New Teaching

(continued)

Don't Forget! Now that you've introduced these three new phonograms, you'll need to include them in your daily letter tile setup.

Point to the <u>ch</u> tile. ch

"This one has three different sounds: /ch/–/k/–/sh/. Repeat after me: / ch/–/k/–/sh/." *Student repeats the sounds.*

"Good. These tiles are called consonant teams. We will add them to our letter tile setup under their own label, Consonant Teams." Help your student organize the new tiles.

Store the new tiles under the following label:

Consonant Teams

th   sh   ch

Take out Phonogram Cards 27-29 and practice them with your student. Show the student the card and have him say the sound.

Phonogram Cards

Teach Sound Cards 27-29

Take out Sound Cards 27-29.

Sound Cards

"I am going to dictate a sound. Write the two letters that work together to make that sound."

Dictate the new Sound Cards.

Practice until your student can easily write down the correct phonograms.

Any time you introduce a new flashcard in a lesson—Phonogram, Sound, Word, or Key Card—remember to file it behind the appropriate **Review** divider in your student's Spelling Review Box. Shuffle the cards before reviewing them with your student.

If your student doesn't hesitate on a flashcard during the daily review, that card is ready to be filed behind the appropriate **Mastered** divider.

Step 9: Short U

Word Cards 31-40: Spell with Tiles

Dictate the words and have your student spell them with tiles. Follow the **Procedure for Spelling with Tiles**, illustrated in Appendix C.

31. **up**
32. **fun**
33. **bug**
34. **sun**   The sun rises in the east.
35. **run**
36. **bus**
37. **dug**   I dug a hole in the yard.
38. **mud**
39. **us**
40. **rug**

Spell on Paper

Once your student is able to spell the words using the tiles, dictate Word Cards 31-40 and have him spell the words on paper.

File the Word Cards behind the Review divider.

More Words

The following words reinforce the concepts taught in Step 9. Have your student spell them for additional practice.

bud	**bun**	**but** (all but one)	**gum**
gun	**hug**	**hum**	**hut**
jug	**mug**	**pup**	**rub**
tub	**tug**	**yum**	

Step 10 – Short E

This lesson will teach how to count syllables and how to spell words containing short e.

You will need: Key Card 6, Word Cards 41-50

Review

Phonogram Cards   Sound Cards   Key Cards   Word Cards

New Teaching

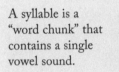

A syllable is a "word chunk" that contains a single vowel sound.

Teach Key Card 6: Counting Syllables

In this next exercise, you will demonstrate what a syllable is by clapping your hands as you say the syllables.

"All words have syllables. A word might have one, two, or even more syllables."

"*Reading* has two syllables: *read* [clap] –*ing* [clap]."
"*Blue* has one syllable: *blue* [clap]."
"*Pumpkin* has two syllables: *pump* [clap] –*kin* [clap]."

"Now you try. Clap your hands for each syllable in the word *pig*."

Have your student practice counting syllables with these words:

seven	**mice**	**hotdog**	**window**	**truck**
paper	**yellow**	**toys**	**elephant**	**swimming**

For further practice, read Key Card 6 with your student and then file it behind the Review divider.

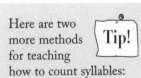

Here are two more methods for teaching how to count syllables:

1. Have the student put his hand under his chin, say the word, and count how many times his jaw drops.

2. Have younger students jump for each "chunk" of the word. Each jump represents one syllable.

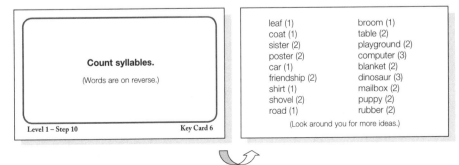

Count syllables.

(Words are on reverse.)

Level 1 – Step 10   Key Card 6

leaf (1)	broom (1)
coat (1)	table (2)
sister (2)	playground (2)
poster (2)	computer (3)
car (1)	blanket (2)
friendship (2)	dinosaur (3)
shirt (1)	mailbox (2)
shovel (2)	puppy (2)
road (1)	rubber (2)

(Look around you for more ideas.)

Word Cards 41-50: Spell with Tiles

Dictate the words and have your student spell them with tiles. Follow the **Procedure for Spelling with Tiles**, illustrated in Appendix C.

41. **yes**
42. **wet**   Why are your shoes wet?
43. **red**   She has seven red balloons.
44. **men**
45. **get**
46. **leg**
47. **pet**
48. **ten**
49. **fed**
50. **pen**

Spell on Paper

Once your student is able to spell the words using the tiles, dictate Word Cards 41-50 and have him spell the words on paper.

File the Word Cards behind the Review divider.

More Words

The following words reinforce the concepts taught in Step 10. Have your student spell them for additional practice.

bed	**beg**	**Ben**	**bet**
Deb	**den**	**Ed**	**hen**
jet	**led** (led a parade)	**let**	**Meg**
met	**net**	**set**	**Ted**
vet	**web**	**yet**	

Step 11 – S, X, and QU

This lesson will teach how to spell words containing x, qu, and the second sound of s.

You will need: Word Cards 51-60

Review

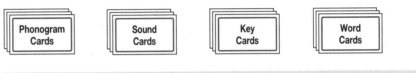

It's time to review the cards behind the **Mastered** dividers to ensure that they stay fresh in your student's mind.

Shuffle the cards behind each Mastered divider and choose a selection for review.

New Teaching

Teach Two Ways to Spell /z/

"We have two ways to spell the sound of /z/. Look at the tiles and see if you can figure out the two ways." *Letters s and z.*

If your student doesn't know the answer, point to the s tile and ask, "What are the two sounds of this tile?" **Tip!**

"Good! Most of the time, when you hear the sound of /z/ at the end of a word, you will use the letter s."

Build the word *has*. | h | a | s |

"What sound do you hear at the end of the word *has*?" /z/.

"What letter did I use to spell the sound of /z/ at the end of the word?" *The s.*

We do use the letter <u>z</u> to represent the sound of /z/ at the end of one common word: *quiz*. *Quiz* will be introduced in a later level, so there will be no confusion when learning the generalization taught in this lesson.

Other words that use the letter <u>z</u> at the end include *buzz, frizz, fuzz, jazz, topaz,* and *whiz*. However, the letter <u>s</u> is used much more frequently to represent the final /z/ sound, such as in the words *wings, changes, waves,* and *was*.

Emphasize the Sounds of Letter Tiles QU and X

Build the word *quit*. | qu | i | t |

"This words says...?" *Quit.*

Point to the <u>qu</u> tile. "When <u>q</u> and <u>u</u> are together, the <u>u</u> doesn't act like a vowel. It works with the <u>q</u> to make the /kw/ sound."

"Say this word: *box*." *Student repeats the word.*

"The /ks/ sound you hear is spelled with an <u>x</u>." | x |

"Spell the word *box*." *Student spells the word with tiles.* | b | o | x |

"<u>X</u> is used in some of today's spelling words. Repeat these words after me and listen for the /ks/ sound that the <u>x</u> makes." Say each word and have the student repeat it:

six   **mix**   **fox**   **fix**   **wax**

Word Cards 51-60: Spell with Tiles

Dictate the words and have your student spell them with tiles. Follow the **Procedure for Spelling with Tiles**, illustrated in Appendix C.

> **51.** as
> **52.** has
> **53.** is
> **54.** his
> **55.** box
> **56.** six
> **57.** mix
> **58.** fox
> **59.** quit
> **60.** fix

Spell on Paper

Once your student is able to spell the words using the tiles, dictate Word Cards 51-60 and have him spell the words on paper.

File the Word Cards behind the Review divider.

Reinforcement

More Words

The following words reinforce the concepts taught in Step 11. Have your student spell them for additional practice.

ox   **tax** (pay a tax)   **wax** (made of wax)

Reinforcement

Dictate Phrases

Starting with this lesson, you will dictate several phrases each day. The phrases reinforce concepts taught in both current and previous lessons. Your student should repeat the phrase and then write it.

Having your student repeat the phrase before he writes it will help him develop a good routine for future lessons.

Later, in Level 2, we will be dictating whole sentences, not just phrases. The sentences are longer, and you will be reading them out loud one time. Repeating the phrases and sentences out loud helps the student remember them more easily and write them down accurately.

big dog

on top

dig in mud

fox den

fix it

mix up

fat cat

his box

quit it

hot sun

six men

sad pig

Step 11: S, X, and QU

Step 12 – TH, SH, and CH

This lesson will teach how to spell words containing digraphs th, sh, and ch.

You will need: four tokens, Word Cards 61-70

Review

Phonogram Cards   Sound Cards   Key Cards   Word Cards

New Teaching

Segment Words

Lay four tokens on the table.

Give your student a word from the following list. He should repeat the word slowly and then say the individual sounds. **As he says each sound,** he pulls a token toward himself, like this:

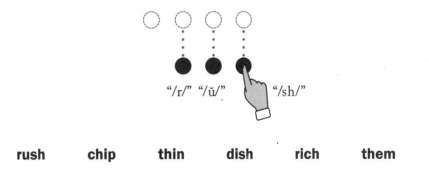

"/r/" "/ŭ/" "/sh/"

rush   **chip**   **thin**   **dish**   **rich**   **them**

Your student will only need three tokens to segment each word, but set out four tokens to encourage him to think through this activity.

Word Cards 61-70: Spell with Tiles

Dictate the words and have your student spell them with tiles. Follow the **Procedure for Spelling with Tiles**, illustrated in Appendix C.

61. fish
62. ship
63. shop
64. much
65. bath
66. this
67. chin
68. math
69. with
70. that

Reinforcement

Spell on Paper

Once your student is able to spell the words using the tiles, dictate Word Cards 61-70 and have him spell the words on paper.

File the Word Cards behind the Review divider.

More Words

The following words reinforce the concepts taught in Step 12. Have your student spell them for additional practice.

Beth	chip	chop	dash	dish
moth	path	rash	rich	rush
shed	shin	shot	shut	such
than	them	then	thin	thud
wish				

Reinforcement
(continued)

Dictate Phrases

Dictate several phrases each day.

fish shop

this bug

fun hat

wet mop

ran with them

bad path

thin moth

hug him

rub his chin

rich man

shut that shed

has an ox

Your student is halfway there! Has he been filling out his Progress Chart?

Step 13 – Segmenting Words with Blends

This lesson will teach how to segment words with final and initial consonant blends.

You will need: four tokens

Today your student is going to learn to segment words with consonant blends.

A **consonant blend** consists of two sounds that are said together quickly, thereby blending together into one sound. For example, the word *lamp* has a consonant blend at the end. The /m/ and /p/ sounds are said together, but each consonant keeps its own sound.

A blend at the end of a word is called a **final blend**, as in *lamp*. A blend at the beginning of a word is called an **initial blend**, as in *plan*.

Review

Phonogram Cards   Sound Cards   Key Cards   Word Cards

New Teaching

Teach How to Segment Words with Final Blends

In this excercise, your student is not spelling these words—he is just segmenting them.

Lay four tokens on the table.

Give your student a word from the following list. He should repeat the word slowly and then say the individual sounds. **As he says each sound,** he pulls a token toward himself, like this:

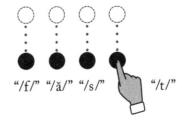

"/f/"   "/ă/"   "/s/"   "/t/"

Words are provided for several practice sessions.

fast	melt	lost	hunt	land
tent	bend	gift	held	hint
west	just	lamp	past	rust
send	rent	soft	left	last
best	hand	went	help	must

Final blends are easier to segment than initial blends. Therefore, make sure that your student can segment the words on the previous list before tackling the words in the next exercise.

Tip!

It is important for your student to know how to segment words before you move on in the lessons. This is the foundation, and good spelling builds upon it. He must learn to hear the individual sounds in words; otherwise, he is just going to be memorizing strings of letters. There are only so many words that a person can learn by sight. It might seem easier at the beginning to learn whole words by sight, but in the long run it is FAR better to know how to spell by sound.

If your student has problems segmenting blends, teach the skill in a concrete way.

Put four sheets of paper on the floor, lined up in a row. Each sheet should be a different color or, if you don't have colored paper, color a big square on each sheet with crayons. You want to be able to differentiate between the four papers.

Part One

Think of a word, like *fast*. Don't tell your student the word. Step on the first paper and say /f/. Step on the second paper and say /ă/. Step on the third paper and say /s/, and then on the fourth and say /t/. Have him guess the word.

Part Two

When your student can easily guess the word, change the game a little. After you've stepped on each piece of paper and said the /f/–/ă/–/s/–/t/ sounds in quick sequence, jump back to the first paper and ask, "What sound was this?" Jump to each paper in turn and have the student identify the corresponding sound. Repeat this with other words until it becomes easy.

Part Three

Next, have your student segment the word himself. Give him a word that you have already done and have him model your example. He will step on the papers, each paper representing one sound.

Part Four

Now your student should have a good grasp on what is required to segment blends. Dictate words from the list and, any time he gets "stuck," model how it should be done and have him imitate you.

Step 13: Segmenting Words with Blends

Teach How to Segment Words with Initial Blends

The following words have a consonant blend at the beginning (**initial blend**).

Dictate each word to your student. He should say the word very slowly, segmenting each individual sound. **As he says each sound,** he pulls down a token.

flip	stop	spin	trip	twig
twin	trim	brush	spot	slip
glad	sled	flag	grip	flop
plug	plum	shred	slam	swim
frog	plan	step	swam	trap

Reinforcement

Dictate Phrases
Dictate several phrases each day.

There are no new
Word Cards for
Step 13.

not yet

log hut

if Beth sat

hum it

much wax

get mad

that bad dog

met us

hot bath

sit in bed

did not rush

fed that hen

Step 14 – Final Blends

This lesson will teach how to spell words with blends at the end.

You will need: Word Cards 71-80

Review

Phonogram Cards   Sound Cards   Key Cards   Word Cards

New Teaching

Word Cards 71-80: Spell with Tiles

Dictate the words and have your student spell them with tiles. Follow the **Procedure for Spelling with Tiles**, illustrated in Appendix C.

71. fast
72. land
73. went
74. soft
75. left
76. last
77. and
78. hand
79. help
80. best

Spell on Paper

Once your student is able to spell the words using the tiles, dictate Word Cards 71-80 and have him spell the words on paper.

File the Word Cards behind the Review divider.

Reinforcement

More Words

The following words reinforce the concepts taught in Step 14. Have your student spell them for additional practice.

band (marching band)	**bend**	**bump**	**dust**
end	**felt**	**gift**	**held**
hint	**hunt**	**its** (wag its tail)	**jump**
just	**lamp**	**lend**	**list**
lost	**melt**	**must** (must do)	**nest**
next	**past** (run past)	**pond**	**raft**
rest	**sand**	**send**	**sent**
sits	**tent**	**test**	**vent**
west	**wind** (breeze)		

Dictate Phrases

Dictate several phrases each day.

best gift

ten men

soft sand

last pet

left hand

run and help

lost ship

fast jog

went past Jim

just rest

at an end

zip it up

Reinforcement
(continued)

When your student misspells a word outside of the spelling lesson, such as when he is doing his own personal writing or completing assignments for another class, hold him responsible for spelling the word correctly if it includes concepts already covered in spelling class.

Tip!

If the word, or a word with a similar pattern, *has* been taught, ask the student to segment the word. As he segments the word aloud he should write down the phonogram for each sound.

Here is another technique: have your student segment the word aloud and draw one blank line for each sound he hears in the word. Then he should go back and fill in the blanks with letters. If the word is *west*, for example, he would draw four blank lines, then fill them in with the letters <u>w</u>, <u>e</u>, <u>s</u>, <u>t</u>.

If a student asks how to spell a word that he has not yet learned, tell him the spelling. Do not encourage "invented spelling" because it only reinforces incorrect spelling that will later have to be relearned.

Step 15 – Initial Blends

This lesson will teach how to spell words with blends at the beginning.

You will need: Word Cards 81-90

Review

New Teaching

Word Cards 81-90: Spell with Tiles

In the following list, make sure your student pronounces the word *trip* carefully and enunciates the <u>t</u>. Otherwise, he may hear the sound of /ch/ in place of the <u>t</u>.

This is common with the <u>tr</u> blend. Listen to the words *try, tree,* and *trick*. In many regions, we hear /ch/ at the beginning of these words in conversational speech.

Dictate the words and have your student spell them with tiles. Follow the **Procedure for Spelling with Tiles**, illustrated in Appendix C.

81. **stop**
82. **glad**
83. **sled**
84. **flag**
85. **frog**
86. **plan**
87. **step** Did she step on your toe?
88. **trip**
89. **swim**
90. **spot**

New Teaching
(continued)

Spell on Paper

Once your student is able to spell the words using the tiles, dictate Word Cards 81-90 and have him spell the words on paper.

File the Word Cards behind the Review divider.

Reinforcement

More Words

The following words reinforce the concepts taught in Step 15. Have your student spell them for additional practice.

brush	drip	drop	flip
grip	plug	plum (eat a plum)	slid
slip	sped	spin	spun
swam	trim	twig	twin

> Pronounce *drip* and *drop* carefully; many children hear and pronounce the d as a j. You may have to remind your student to "pronounce for spelling" and enunciate the d. **Tip!**

Dictate Phrases

Dictate several phrases each day.

must stop

pond frog

flip and spin

step on

hid his plum

west wind

is glad

plan this trip

brush them

drop that sled

swam in jam

then had ham

Reinforcement

(continued)

 Is the daily review helping your student internalize all the concepts he's learned so far? Are the decks behind the Mastered dividers getting bigger? Does your student have a firm grasp on the Key Card rules for spelling?

Mastered cards will be reviewed again in Step 17 to keep them fresh in your student's mind.

Step 16 – Letters C and K

This lesson will teach when to use c and when to use k for the initial sound of /k/.

You will need: Key Cards 7 and 8, blank blue tile

Review

 Phonogram Cards   Sound Cards   Key Cards   Word Cards

New Teaching

Teach Key Card 7: When C Says /s/

Pull down the c tile.   c

"You know that the letter c can say /k/ or /s/. We have a way to tell which of these two sounds the c is going to make."

Pull down the letter tiles e, i, and y and arrange them next to the c tile:

"If the c is followed by an e, i, or y, it says /s/."

Show the c tile visiting the letters e, i, and y one at a time.

"In front of the e it says /s/. In front of the i it says /s/. In front of the y it says /s/."

Pull down the letter tiles a, o, u, l, and r and arrange them like this:

"If the <u>c</u> is before **any other letter**, it says /k/." Show the <u>c</u> tile visiting the letters one at a time.

"In front of the <u>a</u> it says /k/." Repeat for <u>o</u>, <u>u</u>, <u>l</u>, and <u>r</u>.

When your student understands this concept, mix up the <u>e</u>, <u>i</u>, and <u>y</u> with the <u>a</u>, <u>o</u>, <u>u</u>, <u>l</u>, and <u>r</u> and place the <u>c</u> in front of each one. Ask your student to tell you whether the <u>c</u> says /k/ or /s/.

Read Key Card 7 with your student and then file it behind the Review divider.

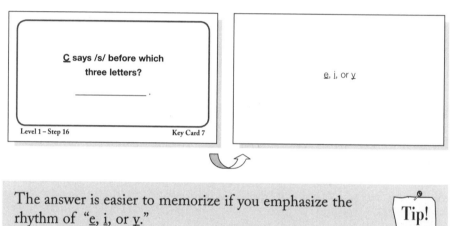

<u>c</u> says /s/ before which
three letters?

_____ .

Level 1 – Step 16   Key Card 7

<u>e</u>, <u>i</u>, or <u>y</u>

The answer is easier to memorize if you emphasize the rhythm of "<u>e</u>, <u>i</u>, or <u>y</u>."   Tip!

The next part of the lesson builds on Key Card 7, so work with the tile activity above until it has been mastered by your student.

Teach Key Card 8: How to Spell the Initial Sound of /k/

Pull down the <u>k</u> tile. [k]

"What sound does this tile make?" */k/.*

"Good. I want to spell the word *kit*. I don't know whether to use the <u>c</u> or the <u>k</u> yet, so I put in a blank blue tile for the /k/ sound."

[ ] [i] [t]   [c]
                [k]

"We always try the <u>c</u> first."

"Does <u>c</u> work?" *No.*

"Why not?" *The c says /s/ because of the i.*

"What would this word say?" /sĭt/.

"So we know that we use the k." 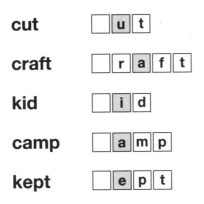 k i t

Build the following words, using a blank blue tile for the /k/ sound. Have your student replace it with a c or a k. Remind him, if necessary, that we always try the c tile first.

cut ☐ u t

craft ☐ r a f t

kid ☐ i d

camp ☐ a m p

kept ☐ e p t

Read Key Card 8 with your student and then file it behind the Review divider.

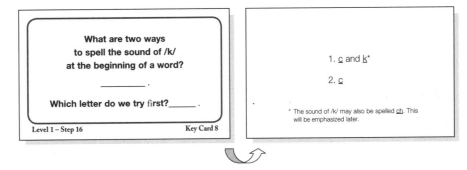

**What are two ways
to spell the sound of /k/
at the beginning of a word?**

_____ .

Which letter do we try first?_____ .

Level 1 – Step 16   Key Card 8

1. c and k*

2. c

* The sound of /k/ may also be spelled ch. This will be emphasized later.

Tip!

Here is an easy way to remember whether to try c first or k first: c comes first in the alphabet and k comes second. That is the same order in which we try the letters when building a word.

C and k are by far the most common ways to spell the sound of /k/ at the beginning of a word. Used much less frequently, ch represents the sound of /k/ in words of Greek origin (*Christmas, chorus*) and will be highlighted in a later level.

Reinforcement

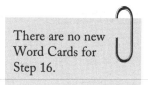

There are no new Word Cards for Step 16.

Dictate Phrases

Dictate several phrases each day.

red flag

Pam and Ted

swim fast

plug in

got that job

twin pig

bit his shin

last wish

hunt with us

held that lamp

felt as bad

trim this twig

Step 17 – Sound of /k/ at the Beginning

This lesson will teach how to spell words beginning with c and k.

You will need: Word Cards 91-100

Review

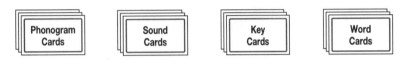

 Quickly review selected cards from behind the **Mastered** dividers.

New Teaching

Word Cards 91-100: Spell with Tiles

Dictate the words and have your student spell them with tiles. Follow the **Procedure for Spelling with Tiles**, illustrated in Appendix C.

91. can
92. camp
93. cut
94. kept
95. kid
96. cash   He paid in cash.
97. kit
98. cup
99. club
100. cap

For each word in this list, have your student pull the blank blue tile down when he hears the sound of /k/. He should spell the rest of the word, then go back and fill it in with either a c or a k.

New Teaching
(continued)

Spell on Paper

Once your student is able to spell the words using the tiles, dictate Word Cards 91-100 and have him spell the words on paper.

File the Word Cards behind the Review divider.

Reinforcement

More Words

The following words reinforce the concepts taught in Step 17. Have your student spell them for additional practice.

cab	**cast** (plaster cast)	**clam**	**cost**	**crab**
crash	**crop**	**cub**	**Ken**	**Kim**

> For the word *cost*, you may have to remind your student to "pronounce for spelling." In many regions, it is pronounced *cawst*.
>
> **Tip!**

Dictate Phrases

Dictate several phrases each day.

Kim sent

kept fit

at camp

drop this cup

tent kit

last crab

that kid

bend and cut

his club

such cost

much cash

Ken can hop

Step 18 – FF, LL, and SS

This lesson will teach three new phonograms and that letters f, l, and s may be doubled at the end of a word.

You will need: letter tiles ck, ng, and nk, Phonogram Cards 30-32, Sound Cards 30-32, Key Card 9, the extra f, l, and s tiles, Word Cards 101-110

Before teaching your student today, review the new Phonogram Cards that you will be presenting in the lesson.

Review

New Teaching

Teach New Phonograms CK, NG, and NK

"We have three new tiles today."

Point to the ck tile. `ck`

"Repeat after me: /k/, two-letter /k/." *Student repeats.*

Point to the ng tile. `ng`

"Repeat after me: /ng/." *Student repeats.*

Point to the nk tile. `nk`

"Repeat after me: /ngk/." *Student repeats.*

"Good. These tiles are consonant teams, so let's put them in the right spot in our letter tile setup." Help your student organize the new tiles.

Store the new tiles under the following label:

Consonant Teams

`ck` `ng` `nk`

New Teaching
(continued)

Take out Phonogram Cards 30-32 and practice them with your student.

Practice Sound Cards 30-32 with your student. Dictate the sound and have your student write the phonogram.

File cards behind the appropriate Review dividers.

Teach Key Card 9: Doubling the Letters F, L, and S

Build the words *off*, *tell*, and *dress* with tiles.

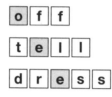

"At the end of one-syllable words, we often double the letters <u>f</u>, <u>l</u>, and <u>s</u> when they come right after a single vowel."

"A **single vowel** means **one vowel**. It means that there aren't two vowels in a row."

Point to the word *off*. "How many syllables are in the word *off*?" *One.*

"Does the <u>f</u> come right after a single vowel?" *Yes.*

Point to the word *tell*. "How many syllables are in the word *tell*?" *One.*

"Does the <u>l</u> come right after a single vowel?" *Yes.*

Point to the word *dress*. "How many syllables are in the word *dress*?" *One.*

"Does the <u>s</u> come right after a single vowel?" *Yes.*

Read Key Card 9 with your student and then file it behind the Review divider.

This rule is sometimes called the **Floss Rule** because the word *floss* follows the rule and contains the letters <u>f</u>, <u>l</u>, and <u>s</u>.

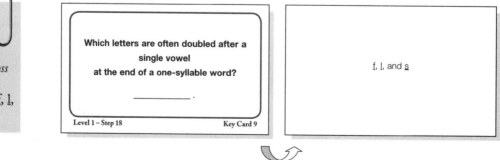

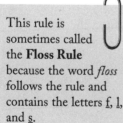

Step 18: FF, LL, and SS

We double the <u>f</u>, <u>l</u>, and <u>s</u> after a single vowel in hundreds of words, but there are several common words in which we do **not** double the last letter. Your student has already learned six of those words: *if, gas, yes, this, us,* and *bus.*

When a final <u>s</u> sounds like /z/, as in *has, was,* and *is,* it is not doubled.

Word Cards 101-110: Spell with Tiles

Dictate the words and have your student spell them with tiles. Follow the **Procedure for Spelling with Tiles**, illustrated in Appendix C.

101. tell

102. doll

103. fell

104. hill

105. will

106. sell   We sell apples.

107. off

108. miss

109. glass

110. grass

> **Tip!**
> For the words *doll* and *off,* you may need to tell your student to "pronounce for spelling." In many regions, the words are pronounced *dawl* and *awf* in conversational speech.

Spell on Paper

Once your student is able to spell the words using the tiles, dictate Word Cards 101-110 and have him spell the words on paper.

File the Word Cards behind the Review divider.

More Words

The following words reinforce the concepts taught in Step 18. Have your student spell them for additional practice.

bell	bill	class	cliff	cuff
dress	drill	fill (fill a cup)	ill	Jill
kill	kiss	less	loss	mess
pass	pill	press	shall	smell
sniff	spell	stiff	still	stuff
well				

Dictate Phrases

Dictate several phrases each day.

fell off

sit still

tell Dan

math class

sniff and smell

fill this glass

rag doll

big cliff

will sell

hug and kiss

best dress

dug that well

Step 19 – Sound of /k/ at the End

This lesson will teach when to use k̲ and c̲k̲ at the end of a one-syllable word.

You will need: Key Card 10, Word Cards 111-120

Review

 Phonogram Cards   Sound Cards   Key Cards   Word Cards

New Teaching

Teach Key Card 10: CK and K at the End of a Word

"Here are two ways to spell /k/ at the end of a word."

Pull down tiles c̲k̲ and k̲.   `ck` `k`

Build the word *rock*, placing a blank blue tile in place of the /k/ sound.   `r` `o` `□`

"I want to spell the word *rock*. In place of this blank tile, I need to decide whether to use the c̲k̲ or the k̲."

"The first thing I have to do is look at the letter that comes **right before** the sound of /k/ and see if it is a short vowel." Point to the o̲.

"Is this a short vowel?" *Yes.*

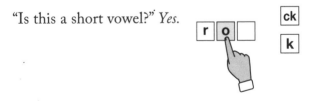

"It is, so we use c̲k̲. Remember that when the sound of /k/ at the end of a word comes **right after** a short vowel, we use c̲k̲."

Replace the blank tile with the c̲k̲ tile.   `r` `o` `ck`

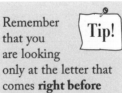
Remember that you are looking only at the letter that comes **right before** the sound of /k/. If it is a short vowel, we use c̲k̲.

Although words like *ask* and *elk* have short vowels, the vowels do **not** come right before the sound of /k/, so we **cannot** use c̲k̲.

New Teaching
(continued)

"Let's try another word. The word I want to spell is *ask*."

"I need to decide whether to use the <u>ck</u> or the <u>k</u>. What should I do first?" *Look at the letter that comes right before the /k/ sound.*

"Right. I need to see if it is a short vowel." Point to the <u>s</u> tile. "Is this a short vowel?" *No.*

"<u>S</u> is not a short vowel, so we use <u>k</u>." | a | s | k |

"So when do we use <u>ck</u> for the sound of /k/ at the end of a word?" *Only when it comes right after a short vowel.*

"Good. Let's try one more word together."

Build the word *elk*, using a blank blue tile for the sound of /k/.

| e | l | □ | | ck |
| | | | | k |

"Does this word have a short vowel in it?" *Yes.*

"Does the short vowel come right before the sound of /k/?" *No.*

"So do we spell the sound of /k/ with <u>ck</u> or <u>k</u> in this word?" *With <u>k</u>.*

"Why?" *Because we only use <u>ck</u> right after a short vowel.*

Have your student practice this concept with several of the following words. Build the word for your student, putting a blank blue tile in place of the /k/ sound.

lock   sick   risk   snack   mask

Step 19: Sound of /k/ at the End

New Teaching
(continued)

Read Key Card 10 with your student and then file it behind the Review divider.

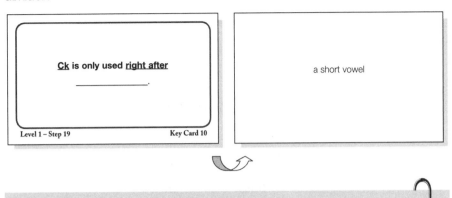

The sound of /k/ at the end of a word can also be spelled:

1. <u>c</u> in multisyllable words ending in -<u>ic</u> *(metric, systemic)* and a small number of less common one-syllable words *(talc, arc)*.

2. <u>ch</u> in words of Greek origin *(stomach, epoch)*.

Words with these spellings will be taught in a later level.

Word Cards 111-120: Spell with Tiles

Dictate the words and have your student spell them with tiles. Follow the **Procedure for Spelling with Tiles**, illustrated in Appendix C.

111. black
112. clock
113. milk
114. duck
115. neck
116. pick
117. ask
118. rock
119. desk
120. snack

New Teaching
(continued)

Spell on Paper

Once your student is able to spell the words using the tiles, dictate Word Cards 111-120 and have him spell the words on paper.

File the Word Cards behind the Review divider.

Reinforcement

More Words

The following words reinforce the concepts taught in Step 19. Have your student spell them for additional practice.

back	block	brick	check	deck
elk	husk	kick	lock (lock the door)	luck
mask	pack	quack	quick	Rick
risk	sick	stick	stuck	task
thick	trick	truck	tuck	

Dictate Phrases

Dictate several phrases each day.

ask Ben

pick up

black mask

red brick

fun trick

thick fog

stiff neck

check them

stuck in mud

hunt elk

quick snack

sick duck

Step 20 – Consonant Team NG

This lesson will teach how to spell words containing ng.

You will need: Word Cards 121-130

Review

 Phonogram Cards   Sound Cards   Key Cards   Word Cards

New Teaching

Teach Consonant Team NG

Arrange these tiles:

"Tile <u>ng</u> can come after <u>a</u>." Slide <u>ng</u> next to the <u>a</u>.

"It can come after <u>i</u>." Slide <u>ng</u> next to the <u>i</u>.

"It can come after <u>o</u>." Slide <u>ng</u> next to the <u>o</u>.

"And it can come after <u>u</u>." Slide <u>ng</u> next to the <u>u</u>.

"But it rarely comes after <u>e</u>." Remove the <u>e</u> tile.

> There are four words that have the combination <u>eng</u>: *English, England, length,* and *strength*. These will be taught in a later level.

New Teaching
(continued)

Word Cards 121-130: Spell with Tiles

Dictate the words and have your student spell them with tiles. Follow the **Procedure for Spelling with Tiles**, illustrated in Appendix C.

121. king

122. long

123. sing

124. thing

125. bring

126. sang

127. stung

128. rang

129. wing

130. swing

> If your student spells *king*, *sing*, *thing*, or *bring* with an e instead of an i, remind him that English words rarely contain the combination eng.
>
> In many regions, it does sound as if there is a long e. Your student will need to "pronounce for spelling" and say these words with an /ĭ/ sound.
>
> **Tip!**

Spell on Paper

Once your student is able to spell the words using the tiles, dictate Word Cards 121-130 and have him spell the words on paper.

File the Word Cards behind the Review divider.

Reinforcement

More Words

The following words reinforce the concepts taught in Step 20. Have your student spell them for additional practice.

bang	hang	hung	ring	song

Reinforcement
(continued)

Dictate Phrases

Dictate several phrases each day.

long nap

sad song

bell rang

less risk

shall sing

on this swing

bring back

it stung Rick

hang up

bat wing

King Ed sang

chop that thing

Step 21 – Consonant Team NK

This lesson will teach how to spell words containing nk.

You will need: Word Cards 131-140

Review

Phonogram Cards   Sound Cards   Key Cards   Word Cards

New Teaching

Teach Consonant Team NK

Arrange these tiles:

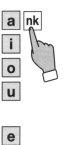

"Tile <u>nk</u> can come after <u>a</u>." Slide <u>nk</u> next to the <u>a</u>.

"It can come after <u>i</u>." Slide <u>nk</u> next to the <u>i</u>.

"It can come after <u>o</u>." Slide <u>nk</u> next to the <u>o</u>.

"And it can come after <u>u</u>." Slide <u>nk</u> next to the <u>u</u>.

"But it never comes after <u>e</u>." Remove the <u>e</u> tile.

Word Cards 131-140: Spell with Tiles

Dictate the words and have your student spell them with tiles. Follow the **Procedure for Spelling with Tiles**, illustrated in Appendix C.

131. bank
132. thank
133. drink
134. pink
135. sink
136. think
137. shrunk
138. trunk
139. sank
140. Frank

Make sure your student pronounces the word *drink* carefully and enunciates the <u>d</u>. Many children pronounce the <u>dr</u> blend as /jr/.

Similarly, your student may need to "pronounce for spelling" the word *trunk* to avoid a /ch/ sound at the beginning.

If your student spells *drink*, *pink*, *sink*, or *think* with an <u>e</u> instead of an <u>i</u>, remind him that English words never contain the combination <u>enk</u>.

Tip!

In many regions, it does sound as if there is a long <u>e</u>. Your student will need to "pronounce for spelling" and say these words with an /ĭ/ sound.

Spell on Paper

Once your student is able to spell the words using the tiles, dictate Word Cards 131-140 and have him spell the words on paper.

File the Word Cards behind the Review divider.

Reinforcement

More Words

The following words reinforce the concepts taught in Step 21. Have your student spell them for additional practice.

blank	drank	dunk	honk	ink
junk	rank	rink	shrank	shrink
sunk	tank			

Dictate Phrases

Dictate several phrases each day.

pink dish

sell junk

black ink

thank them

truck trunk

drank milk

blank spot

fish tank

did not think

ship sank

Frank will win

kick this rock

Step 22 – Compound Words

This lesson will teach how to spell compound words.

You will need: the second set of letter tiles a to z, Word Cards 141-150

When you set out the tiles today, place the new tiles under the first set, like this:

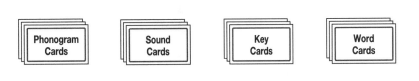

Review

| Phonogram Cards | Sound Cards | Key Cards | Word Cards |

Quickly review selected cards from behind the **Mastered** dividers.

New Teaching

Teach Compound Words

Build the word *sunset*.

"A compound word is two smaller words put together. What are the two small words in the word *sunset*?" *Sun, set.*

"How many syllables are in the word *sunset*?" *Two.*

"To spell a two-syllable word, clap it out." Show how to do this. Clap as you say *sun*, then clap as you say *set*.

"Spell the first syllable, *sun*."

"Then spell the second syllable, *set*."

"Then we double-check the word to make sure that we spelled it correctly." Say the word slowly while running your finger under the word.

Word Cards 141-150: Spell with Tiles

Dictate the words and have your student spell them with tiles. Follow the **Procedure for Spelling with Tiles**, illustrated in Appendix C.

141. bathtub
142. within
143. sunset
144. cobweb
145. itself
146. desktop
147. himself
148. upset
149. windmill
150. bobcat

Spell on Paper

Once your student is able to spell the words using the tiles, dictate Word Cards 141-150 and have him spell the words on paper.

File the Word Cards behind the Review divider.

Reinforcement

More Words

The following words reinforce the concepts taught in Step 22. Have your student spell them for additional practice.

backpack	blacktop	cannot	catfish
catnip	clamshell	dishcloth	drumstick
gunshot	handcuff	hilltop	hotdog
lipstick	locksmith	milkman	pigpen
quicksand	shellfish	upon	

Reinforcement

Dictate Phrases

Dictate several phrases each day.

wet dishcloth

red sunset

upset the bobcat

pink lipstick

milkman left

long cobweb

quack at Sam

upon this hilltop

cannot lock it

in his backpack

let himself in

sink in quicksand

Step 23 – Plural Words

This lesson will teach how to spell plural words by adding s or es.

You will need: third s letter tile, Key Cards 11-13, Word Cards 151-160

Review

Phonogram Cards   Sound Cards   Key Cards   Word Cards

New Teaching

Teach Key Card 11: Plurals

Build the word *bugs* with the tiles.

"We say one *bug*—"
(Cover the s with your finger.)

"—and we say two *bugs*."

"*Bugs* is **plural** because it means **more than one**."

Read Key Card 11 with your student and then file it behind the Review divider.

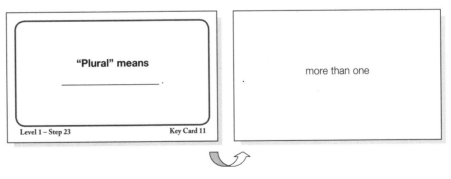

New Teaching
(continued)

"I'll say a word and you make it plural."

"One *cat*, two _____." If necessary, prompt your student to say *cats*.

"One *tent*, two _____." *Tents.*

"One *ball*, five _____." *Balls.*

Teach Key Cards 12 and 13: Adding S and ES and Identifying Base Words

"Now we are going to do just the opposite. I will tell you the **plural word** (like *swings*), and you will tell me the **base word** (*swing*)."

"The word is *chairs*." *Chair.*

Repeat this exercise until your student can easily identify the base word. Practice with the following words. Your student is not spelling these words; he is only giving you the base word verbally.

books	**plants**	**benches**	**walls**	**pencils**
cows	**cups**	**coats**	**cars**	

"Let's build some words. I want to spell the word *maps*."

"First I build the base word, *map*." m a p

"Next, I pull down an s."

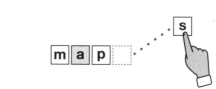

"The next word is *frogs*. First I build the base word, *frog*."

f r o g

"Then I add s to make it say *frogs*."

104

New Teaching
(continued)

Pull down the z̲ tile and place it over the s̲ tile in the word *frogs*. "Even though we hear the sound of /z/ in *frogs*, we never use the z̲ tile to make a word plural."

| f | r | o | g | z |

"We use the second sound of s̲ in this word."

| f | r | o | g | s |

Show this concept using the words *hands*, *pigs*, and *dolls*.

Notice how the sound of /d/ in the word *hand* disappears when you say the plural form? *Hand, hands.* By spelling the base word first, your student will include the d̲.

Tip!

If you hear a new syllable when the word is made plural, use e̲s̲ to form the plural.

For example, when the word *glass* is made plural, we hear a second syllable: /glass/–/es/. That is a clue that the plural is fomed by adding e̲s̲.

"I want to spell the word *glasses*."

"*Glasses* is a two-syllable word." Clap out *glass-es.*

"First I spell the first syllable, the base word, *glass.*"

| g | l | a | s | s |

"Then I spell the second syllable, /ez/."

| g | l | a | s | s | e | s |

Show this concept using the words *brushes*, *boxes*, and *classes.* Clap the syllables before spelling the word.

Additional ways to form plurals, such as changing the word (*child* to *children*) and changing the y̲ to i̲ (*fly* to *flies*) will be taught in a later level.

Read Key Card 12 with your student and then file it behind the Review divider.

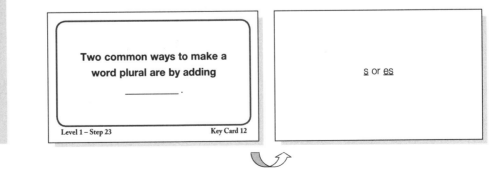

Two common ways to make a word plural are by adding _____ .

Level 1 – Step 23   Key Card 12

s̲ or e̲s̲

Practice some of the words on Key Card 13, then file it behind the Review divider.

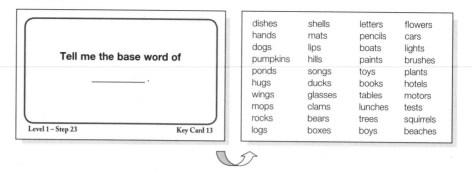

dishes	shells	letters	flowers
hands	mats	pencils	cars
dogs	lips	boats	lights
pumpkins	hills	paints	brushes
ponds	songs	toys	plants
hugs	ducks	books	hotels
wings	glasses	tables	motors
mops	clams	lunches	tests
rocks	bears	trees	squirrels
logs	boxes	boys	beaches

Tell me the base word of

————.

Level 1 – Step 23   Key Card 13

Word Cards 151-160: Spell with Tiles

Dictate the words and have your student spell them with tiles. Follow the **Procedure for Spelling with Tiles**, illustrated in Appendix C.

151. cups

152. beds

153. dishes

154. tents   We pitched our tents in the woods.

155. spots

156. songs

157. dresses

158. trucks

159. rugs

160. desks

> For each word on this list, have your student write down the base word first and then make it plural.

Spell on Paper

Once your student is able to spell the words using the tiles, dictate Word Cards 151-160 and have him spell the words on paper.

File the Word Cards behind the Review divider.

Reinforcement

More Words

The following words reinforce the concepts taught in Step 23. Have your student spell them for additional practice.

backpacks	banks	bats	bells
boxes	bugs	cats	clams
classes	clocks	dogs	dolls
ducks	flags	frogs	gifts
glasses	hats	hens	hills
jobs	kings	kisses	lamps
logs	maps	pigs	plums (ate six plums)
pups	rams	rocks	shells
ships	snacks	things	tracks
trips	twigs	wings	wishes

Dictate Phrases

Dictate several phrases each day.

his glasses

bugs in rugs

camp in tents

pack dishes

ten pink pigs

hung clocks

Bob has hens

cash in banks

get us dresses

snacks in boxes

fill up cups

six sad clams

Step 24 – Open Syllables

This lesson will teach the long vowel sounds, the definition of open and closed syllable types, and how to spell words with open syllables.

You will need: Key Cards 14-16, Word Cards 161-170

Up to this point, your student has worked only with **closed** syllables (where a vowel is followed by a consonant and is generally short). In Level 2, **open** syllables will be used to form multisyllable words. Although the spelling words in this lesson are very easy, the concepts are important.

Review

New Teaching

Teach Key Card 14: Long Vowel Sounds

Put the letter tiles <u>a</u>, <u>e</u>, <u>i</u>, <u>o</u>, and <u>u</u> in front of the student.

Point to the <u>a</u> tile. | a |

"Tell me the three sounds of this letter." /ă/–/ā/–/ah/.

"Which of those sounds is the **short** sound?" /ă/ (or *the first sound*).

"Good. The first sound of a vowel is its short sound. We also have a name for the **second** sound of a vowel. The second sound is called its **long** sound."

"What is the second sound of the letter <u>a</u>?" /ā/.

Point to the e̲ tile. **e**

"What are the two sounds of this letter?" /ĕ/–/ē/.

"What is the long sound of this letter?" /ē/.

Point to the i̲ tile. **i**

"What are the three sounds of this letter?" /ĭ/–/ī/–/ē/.

"What is the long sound of this letter?" /ī/.

Point to the o̲ tile. **o**

Your student can probably see the pattern now.

"And what do you think the long sound of o̲ is?" /ō/.

"And the long sound of u̲ is?" /ū/. **u**

"Good. The long sound of a letter is the same as its name."

Read Key Card 14 with your student and then file it behind the Review divider.

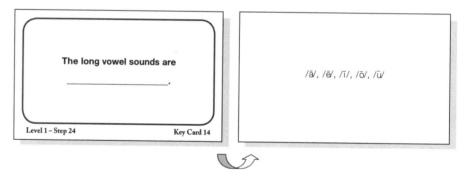

Teach Key Cards 15 and 16: Closed and Open Syllables

Build the word *shed*.

"Point to the vowel."
Student points to the e̲. **sh** **e** **d**

"Is there anything after the e̲?" *Yes, d̲.*

"Good. We say that the e̲ is closed in by the d̲. This is a **closed** syllable."

"Is the vowel in this word short or long?" *Short.*

New Teaching
(continued)

"Right. When a vowel is in a **closed** syllable, it usually says its **short** sound."

Remove the <u>d</u> tile. sh e

"Is there anything after the <u>e</u> now?" *No.*

"We can say that the <u>e</u> is **open**, because there is nothing closing it in."

"When a vowel is in an **open** syllable, it usually says its **long** sound."

Point to the <u>e</u>. "What does the <u>e</u> say in this word?" /ē/.

"This word says…?" *She.*

Build the following words. Have your student tell you whether the syllable is **open** or **closed**.

he	*Open.*
hem	*Closed.*
so	*Open.*
sock	*Closed.*
got	*Closed.*

For additional practice, use the following words:

go	**wet**	**we**	**no**	**not**
I	**it**	**bed**	**be**	

Read Key Cards 15 and 16 with your student and then file them behind the Review divider.

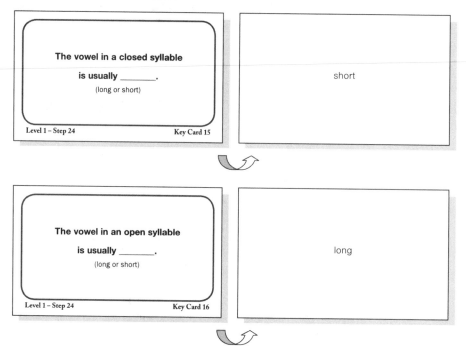

Teach Common Words *The* and *A*

"Here is an interesting case." Build the word *them*.   th e m

"This word says…?" *Them.*

"Remove the <u>m</u> and it says…?" *Student may say /thē/ or /thŭ/.*

"Good. This word can say /thē/or /thŭ/. Usually, we say /thŭ/."

We usually pronounce *the* like /thŭ/. But sometimes we pronounce it as /thē/ when:

1. it comes before a vowel sound *(the apple, the open door, the ice cream).*

2. we want to emphasize something *("You saw THE Queen of England?!").*

For many children, spelling the word *the* doesn't present difficulties because they have seen it in writing so many times. But if your student does have trouble, tell him to "pronounce for spelling" and say it like /thē/ for spelling purposes.

Build the word *a*. a

"The same thing with the word *a*. We can say /ā/ or /uh/ when we speak, and we spell it a̲."

Word Cards 161-170: Spell with Tiles

Dictate the words and have your student spell them with tiles. Follow the **Procedure for Spelling with Tiles**, illustrated in Appendix C.

> **The spelling list in this lesson may be too easy for your student.** If so, show your student that open syllables can be combined with closed syllables to form longer words, such as *begin, event,* and *hero*. (These words will be taught in Level 2.)

161. she

162. we   We ate all the raisins.

163. so   It was so windy that my hat blew off!

164. a

165. he

166. the

167. no   There are no ripe bananas.

168. me

169. be   The dessert will be good.

170. go

Spell on Paper

Once your student is able to spell the words using the tiles, dictate Word Cards 161-170 and have him spell the words on paper.

File the Word Cards behind the Review divider.

Reinforcement

Dictate Phrases

Dictate several phrases each day.

so much gum

fell with a thud

grass on the hill

no bells

in the bathtub

a bad smell

Dictate Sentences

Dictate several sentences each day. If necessary, explain to your student that each sentence will begin with a capital letter and end with a period.

She had six hats.

We sang songs.

He has spots.

Get me a jug.

Go with me.

It will be fun.

Celebrate!

Present Your Student with the Certificate of Achievement

3

Appendices

Scope and Sequence of Level 1

By the end of Level 1, your student will be able to spell most one-syllable words with a short vowel. We take small incremental steps to accomplish this. Skills are introduced one at a time and are continually reviewed. The carefully sequenced activities your student will complete are outlined in the following chart.

Your Student Will:	Step	Your Student Will:	Step
Learn the first 26 phonograms	1	Spell words containing s, x, and qu	11
Identify the first sound in a word	2	Spell words containing th, sh, and ch	12
Identify the last sound in a word	2	Segment words with consonant blends	13
Segment words with two and three sounds	2	Spell words with final blends	14
Alphabetize the letter tiles	3	Spell words with initial blends	15
Distinguish between vowels and consonants	3	Learn that c says /s/ before an e, i, or y	16
Learn how to write the phonograms	4	Learn how to spell /k/ at the beginning of word	16
Learn the short vowel sounds	5	Spell words with c or k at the beginning	17
Choose the correct vowel for a word	5	Learn phonograms ck, ng, and nk	18
Learn that every word has a vowel	5	Learn when to double f, l, and s	18
Exchange vowels to make new words	5	Spell words ending in f, l, and s	18
Segment words with letter tiles	6	Learn how to spell /k/ at the end of a word	19
Learn procedure for spelling with tiles	6	Spell words with ck or k at the end	19
Spell words containing short a	6	Spell words with ng	20
Spell words containing short i	7	Spell words with nk	21
Learn how to capitalize names	8	Spell compound words	22
Spell words containing short o	8	Learn what a plural word is	23
Learn phonograms th, sh, and ch	9	Identify the base word of plural words	23
Spell words containing short u	9	Learn how to make a word plural	23
Understand what a syllable is	10	Spell plural words by adding s or es	23
Count syllables in a word	10	Learn the long vowel sounds	24
Spell words containing short e	10	Learn open and closed syllable types	24
Learn two ways to spell /z/	11	Spell words with open syllables	24

Phonograms are letters or letter combinations that represent a single sound. For example, the letter b represents the sound /b/, as in *bat*. The letter combination sh represents the sound /sh/, as in *ship*.

Card #	Phonogram	Sound	For the Teacher's Use Only (example of word containing the phonogram)			
INTRODUCED IN STEP 1						
1	a	/ă/–/ā/–/ah/	apple	acorn	water	
2	b	/b/	bat			
3	c	/k/–/s/	cat	city		
4	d	/d/	dog			
5	e	/ĕ/–/ē/	Eddy	even		
6	f	/f/	fan			
7	g	/g/–/j/	goat	gem		
8	h	/h/	hat			
9	i	/ĭ/–/ī/–/ē/	igloo	ivy	radio	
10	j	/j/	jam			
11	k	/k/	king			
12	l	/l/	look			
13	m	/m/	map			
14	n	/n/	nest			
15	o	/ŏ/–/ō/–/o͞o/–/ŭ/	odd	open	to	oven
16	p	/p/	pig			
17	qu	/kw/	queen			
18	r	/r/	ran			
19	s	/s/–/z/	sun	has		
20	t	/t/	tap			
21	u	/ŭ/–/ū/–/o͞o/	up	unit	put	
22	v	/v/	vine			
23	w	/w/	we			
24	x	/ks/	box			
25	y	/y/–/ĭ/–/ī/–/ē/	yarn	gym	my	happy
26	z	/z/	zoo			

Card #	Phonogram	Sound	For the Teacher's Use Only (example of word containing the phonogram)		
			INTRODUCED IN STEP 9		
27	th	/th/–/t̶h̶/*	three	then	
28	sh	/sh/	ship		
29	ch	/ch/–/k/–/sh/	child	school	chef
			INTRODUCED IN STEP 18		
30	ck	/k/	duck		
31	ng	/ng/	king		
32	nk	/ngk/	thank		

*You will notice that there is a strikethrough on the /t̶h̶/. This is to differentiate the two different sounds of th. If you teach reading, you may have come across the terms *voiced* and *unvoiced*. The /t̶h̶/ is considered *voiced* and the /th/ is considered *unvoiced*. This terminology is not important for the student to learn, but it helps us as teachers to indicate which sound the th is making.

APPENDIX C
Procedure for Spelling with Tiles

The following routine is very effective and will be used throughout the *All About Spelling* series.

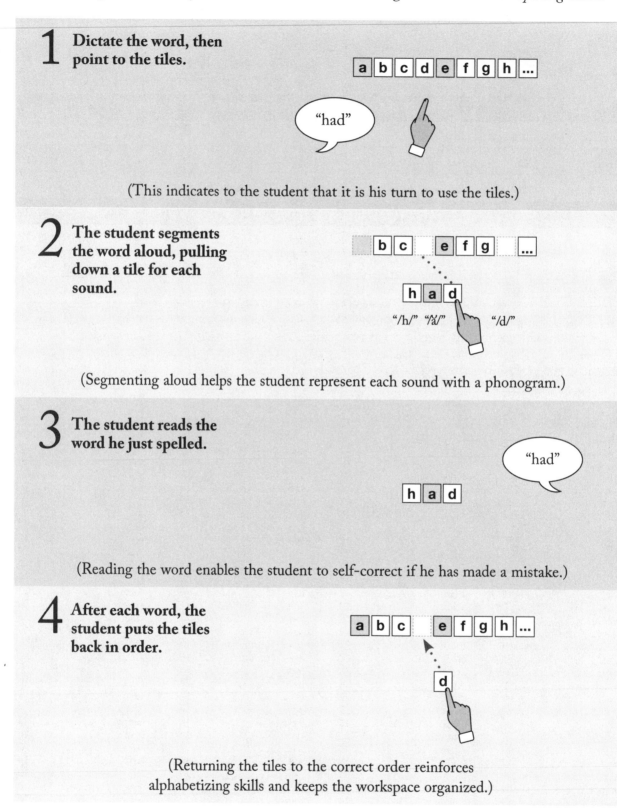

1 **Dictate the word, then point to the tiles.**

"had"

(This indicates to the student that it is his turn to use the tiles.)

2 **The student segments the word aloud, pulling down a tile for each sound.**

h a d

"/h/" "/ă/" "/d/"

(Segmenting aloud helps the student represent each sound with a phonogram.)

3 **The student reads the word he just spelled.**

"had"

h a d

(Reading the word enables the student to self-correct if he has made a mistake.)

4 **After each word, the student puts the tiles back in order.**

(Returning the tiles to the correct order reinforces alphabetizing skills and keeps the workspace organized.)

The number listed corresponds with the Step in which the word is first introduced.

A
a. 24
am 6
an. 6
and. 14
as 11
ask 19
at 6

B
back 19
backpack 22
backpacks. 23
bad. 6
bag. 6
band. 14
bang. 20
bank. 21
banks 23
bat 6
bath 12
bathtub 22
bats 23
be. 24
bed. 10
beds 23
beg. 10
bell. 18
bells 23
Ben 10
bend. 14
best 14
bet 10
Beth. 12
big 7
bill 18
bit 7
black 19
blacktop. 22
blank 21
block 19
Bob 8
bobcat 22
box. 11
boxes 23
brick. 19
bring 20
brush 15
bud. 9
bug. 9
bugs. 23
bump 14
bun 9
bus. 9
but. 9

C
cab 17
camp 17
can. 17
cannot 22
cap. 17
cash 17

cast. 17
cat 6
catfish 22
catnip. 22
cats. 23
check 19
chin 12
chip 12
chop. 12
clam 17
clams 23
clamshell 22
class 18
classes 23
cliff 18
clock 19
clocks 23
club 17
cobweb. 22
cost 17
crash 17
crop 17
cub. 17
cuff 18
cup. 17
cups 23
cut 17

D
dad. 6
Dan 8
dash 12
Deb 10
deck 19
den 10
desk 19
desks 23
desktop 22
did 7
dig 7
dim 7
dish 12
dishcloth 22
dishes. 23
dog. 8
dogs 23
doll. 18
dolls 23
dot. 8
drank 21
dress. 18
dresses 23
drill 18
drink 21
drip 15
drop 15
drumstick. 22
duck. 19
ducks 23
dug. 9
dunk 21
dust 14

E
Ed 19
elk 19
end. 14

F
fan 6
fast. 14
fat 6
fed 10
fell 18
felt 14
fill 18
fish. 12
fit. 7
fix 11
flag. 15
flags 23
flip 15
fog 8
fox 11
Frank 21
frog 15
frogs. 23
fun 9

G
gas 6
get 10
gift 14
gifts 23
glad 15
glass. 18
glasses 23
go. 24
God 8
got 8
grass. 18
grip 15
gum 9
gun. 9
gunshot 22

H
had. 6
ham 6
hand. 14
handcuff 22
hang. 20
has 11
hat 6
hats 23
he. 24
held 14
help 14
hen 10
hens 23
hid 7
hill 18
hills 23
hilltop 22
him 7
himself. 22

hint 14
hip 7
his 11
hit 7
honk 21
hop 8
hot. 8
hotdog. 22
hug. 9
hum 9
hung 20
hunt. 14
husk. 19
hut 9

I
I. 24
if 7
ill 18
in 7
ink 21
is 11
it 7
its. 14
itself. 22

J
jam. 6
jet. 10
Jill 18
Jim. 8
job 8
jobs 23
jog 8
jug 9
jump 14
junk 21
just. 14

K
Ken 17
kept 17
kick 19
kid 17
kill 18
Kim 17
king 20
kings 23
kiss. 18
kisses 23
kit 17

L
lab 6
lamp. 14
lamps 23
land. 14
lap 6
last 14
led 10
left 14
leg 10